A FAITH FOR TEENAGERS

A FAITH FOR TEENAGERS

Making Sense Of Life

JOHN KATER

Published in the United States of America by Cowley
Publications.

International Standard Book No.: 0-936384-51-4

Cover photograph by Jessica A. Boyatt

Library of Congress Cataloging-in-Publication Data

Kater, John.
    A faith for teenagers.

    Summary: A guide to Christian faith and lifestyle for
teenagers.
    1. Youth--Religious life. [1. Christian life]
I. Title.
BV4531.2.K38 1987   248.8'3   87-15701
ISBN 0-936384-51-4

Cowley Publications
980 Memorial Drive
Cambridge, MA 02138

To the people of Christ Episcopal Church

Poughkeepsie, New York

companions on the Way

Acknowledgments

I am grateful to all those who have contributed to the writing, revision, and preparation of this book. Avery Brooke and Don Kraus provided both the original impetus and ongoing guidance which led to its preparation. I wish to thank John M. Palmer, III, Trinity Church, New York City and David W. Perry, All Saints Church, Pasadena for reading the material with a critical eye. I am especially indebted to Michael A. Phillips, my colleague at Christ Church, Poughkeepsie for innumerable suggestions and revisions, and to a group of teenagers at the church who met with me over a period of several months, read the original draft, and gave their encouragement as well as their unique perspective.

A. Lillian Easton and Beth Rabenda provided their customary reliable care in the preparation of the manuscript.

John Kater
Panama, 1987

Cowley Publications is a work of the Society of St. John the Evangelist, a religious community for men in the Episcopal Church. The books we publish are a significant part of our ministry, together with the work of preaching, spiritual direction, and hospitality. Our aim is to provide books that will enrich their readers' religious experience as well as challenge it with fresh approaches to religious concerns.

Contents

Prologue

When Christians become members of the church through baptism, they make a series of promises which are called the baptismal covenant. The questions and answers to the covenant form the heart of what Christian people believe about God, the world, and themselves.

This book explores those promises and some of their implications for teenagers who are investigating Christian faith. You will find a variety of formats here. There are anecdotes, based on the kinds of experiences we have all had, which illustrate or challenge those beliefs. There are questions for you to ask yourself and discuss with friends, reflections about what Christian people believe, now and in the past, and selections from the Bible and the religious literature of other peoples.

I have tried to make this book clear, honest, and straightforward. At times you might think that some of its material is over-simplified. But don't be deceived, because the issues raised are neither simple nor trivial. They are as complex as life itself.

Some people consider religion boring. I don't. I consider it a matter of life and death, and I also believe that discovering the meaning of our life is a challenge and an adventure. I hope that by the time you reach the end of this book you will agree.

PART ONE

Do you believe in God the Father?
I believe in God the Father almighty,
creator of heaven and earth.

Do you believe in Jesus Christ, the Son of God?
I believe in Jesus Christ, his only Son, our Lord.
He was conceived by the power of the Holy
Spirit and born of the Virgin Mary.
He suffered under Pontius Pilate,
was crucified, died, and was buried.
He descended to the dead.
On the third day he rose again.
He ascended into heaven,
and is seated at the right hand of the Father.
He will come again to judge the living
and the dead.

Do you believe in God the Holy Spirit?
I believe in the Holy Spirit,
the holy catholic Church,
the communion of saints,
the forgiveness of sins,
the resurrection of the body,
and the life everlasting.

Our Watery Beginnings

In the year 1844, my great-great-grandfather, whose name (like mine) was John Kater, married a teenager named Margaret Graham. They lived in a little town not far from Glasgow, Scotland. Soon afterwards, they decided that the future there did not hold much promise for a young family, so they decided to come to the United States. Never having traveled anywhere in their lives, they booked passage on a sailing ship bound for Philadelphia. It was a small boat, and it made several stops in Canada and New England before it delivered them at last to their destination. Many years later, my family still remembered their stories of that journey. It took many weeks. There were terrible storms, and at times they were almost positive the ship would never reach land.

Food and water ran low. Many of the people were sick for almost the entire voyage; one or two even died.

I wonder, though, if the physical agony of that sea voyage was as hard to bear as my ancestors' thoughts as the ship carried them farther and farther from their homeland. They knew that they would never see their family again. The trip was too long and hard; their parents too old; and so the farewells they said were final ones. John and Margaret were right. They settled in America, and never again saw the land of their birth, or the people they loved. The ocean was a great barrier over which they had sailed in hope and sadness.

§

My friend Alice Yang knows a similar story about how her family came to America, because her grandparents have told it to her themselves. Her grandfather remembers that his father lived in a very large city in China, and that he heard that there were jobs waiting in a place called America. He was planning to be married to a woman from the same neighborhood, and the job seemed like the chance they were waiting for. He signed up to go to America. When he arrived, things were very different than he had expected. The job was building a railroad in California, the work was hard and the pay was so low that his dream of sending money home so that his fiancee could join him never came true. They wrote for two years, and then one day he received a letter saying that she would not wait any longer. She was engaged to marry someone else.

Later, Alice Yang's ancestor met someone who had come from the same city as he, and they were eventually married. They never learned to speak English, and lived in an apartment house owned by a man from their Chinese birthplace. But their son, Alice's grandfather, not only learned English, but started a small business for himself. Alice has been learning about her family from her grandparents, and hopes to visit China so that she can see for herself where her family once lived.

My friend Alice and I come from very different backgrounds, but our families have had the same kind of experience in their history. Both set out on long journeys from which they could never return. Both crossed the ocean, great bodies of water which divided the place of their birth from the country they eventually came to call home. The sea served as a dividing line between past and present, the old world and the new. Once across the sea, they could never go back to the old world they had left behind.

Many people connect the story of their life's journey with water. The Hebrews, our ancient ancestors in faith, fled through the sea to escape their oppressors. It is not so far-fetched to imagine my great-great-grandparents thinking of that story when they set out for America to find a land of promise and hope. For them, crossing the sea – passing through the water – was the way by which they found what they were looking for, just as the Hebrews crossed the sea in search of their promised land.

But water is more than a barrier, or an obstacle to be crossed in search of new beginnings. It is a rich symbol of what it means to be human.

§

Scientists tell us that life began in the ocean. Millions of years ago – so long ago it stretches our memories beyond their limits – the warm sea gave birth. Perhaps to chemists that moment would seem like any other chemical reaction – the kind you produce in the science lab, or when you add a pinch of salt to a pot of soup. There was something absolutely unique about that split-second in time. Life began. Not that we, or anyone else, could have seen it. The first stirrings of life were far too small to be visible to the naked eye. The earth continued its spinning for centuries and thousands of centuries before living things reached the size we could perceive. And what a journey it was from the single cell to the complexity of tiny creatures of the sea, from microscopic plants to the giant sponges and spectacular coral that grow unnoticed on the ocean floor. What a marvel it must have been for creatures to climb, year by year and century by century, toward the possibility of living outside the sea. What miracles happened to create reptiles, mammals, the great apes, our own long-ago ancestors, and at last, the creatures we call *human*!

Yet each one of us recreates the story of the human family in our own lifetime. The split-second of our conception calls life into being, and in the nine months before our birth we are at home in a tiny sea – our mother's womb. Early in our development, we looked for all the world like a creature of the sea. We were well equipped for a liquid environment, and it was only as the day of our birth grew nearer that we began to develop the limbs and organs that would serve us as male and female members of the human race. We never even breathed the air until the day we left the womb. That was a surprise that awaited us until we had lived through the speeded-up history of our ancestory.

You could really say that the sea is our place of origin. Life got its start in the water, and we also experienced the first stages of life in a watery setting.

If life comes from the water, it also depends on water for its survival. All around the world, there are vast regions that once were covered with forest and

[7]

grassland, where now the land is desert. As recently as your grandparents' day, the Middle West in the United States was known as the "Dust Bowl." Many of the people who now live on the West Coast are the descendants of people who went there during the 1930's because the land their families had farmed for many years became dry and useless. Drought reduced what had been a vast agricultural region to barren wasteland. The same things happened in Africa a few years ago. Millions of people starved in the Sahel region because the land became so dry that animals died and no crop survived.

No wonder water has always been a symbol of life. Our Hebrew ancestors understood that creation begins with water. This is how they told it:

In the beginning of God's creating the heavens and the earth, the earth was formless and empty, and darkness was upon the face of the deep. The Spirit of God was moving over the face of the waters.

Of course, these long-ago story-tellers had no scientific understanding of how life came to be. But they grasped that it began with God's creative presence calling life into being from the sea.

And how mysterious the ocean is, how fascinating it remains. At times, warmed by the sun, it laps at our feet, bringing a calm, lazy feeling to the whole world. At night, the sea is dark, unfathomable. At all times it is beyond understanding, vast, and ever stretching far beyond our vision. Before such power we stand in wonder. It is as if we could hear and touch something of the primal energy of the universe. But always we are attracted to the sea. Some people long to return to its depths, and spend hours learning to master the equipment and the skills necessary to dive to the ocean floor. They are rewarded with a view of the universe that no other human beings can share: creatures of the sea whose beauty is hidden in the dark depths, thrilling and vast creatures like some imaginary monsters which lumber past or peer ominously at their distant cousins from the dry land.

The people of Israel, who are our spiritual ancestors, were not the only ancient people to revere the sea as the womb from which all life came. Almost every people tells and retells a story – or many stories – which show the same honor for the mysterious water which cradles and nourishes life.

And what is more refreshing on a hot summer day than to plunge into the cold ocean, or a pool or river? It is as if the steamy, sweaty discomfort disappears by magic. We are cleansed and renewed. The whole of nature experiences the same washing. A sudden thunderstorm freshens the humid air and makes the natural world bright and green. Or a rare cloudburst descends on the desert, bringing its plants into vivid blossom.

But the sea has another side; water is a complex mystery. In storms, the ocean turns dark and ominous, and its waves are capable of carrying away everything before them. If you have ever seen the after-effects of a hurricane, you know how much power can be unleashed by the waves. The rain, which begins as a spring shower, settling the dust and making things spring to life, can turn into a torrent. Rivers can overflow their banks and become forces of disaster. Whole towns and cities can be laid waste when rivers go on rampage. The treasures of many lifetimes can be washed away in a moment. Confronting the mystery of water is fascinating, but also risky. People drown. People are washed out to sea. People are lost and never found. Water, the source of all life, is also treacherous and demands respect if it is not to turn and destroy us.

When the people of Israel were slaves in Egypt, they suffered for many years until Moses persuaded the Pharaoh to let his people go. Their path took them through the sea and safely to the other side. From that time the sea has been the sign of freedom. When the colonists began to settle North America, they often compared themselves to the people of Israel because both had fled from oppression across the sea to a new land, a land of promise. The sea, which was such a difficult foe when the wind blew their tiny ships off course and lengthened the misery of their voyage into weeks and months, also provided them with safety. They knew that the sea lay between them and their enemies. The sea that had brought them to safety now protected them.

§

People have always known there was something special about the sea. Here is a poem from the Indian people of Colombia:

First there was the sea.
There was neither father nor mother.
The sea was father and mother.

Most peoples seem to preserve some sort of memory of their watery beginnings. But it was not until modern science learned how to break matter down and analyse it that we learned that most of our body is made up of water. Water is our origin, and it makes us who we are. It is the sign of life, and the setting for life.

It is water that Christians use to mark who we are. In the service of baptism, water is poured over our head or we are dipped bodily into a river, stream or pool. In either case, the church is using the most basic symbol of life in the service.

§

Christians believe that the most basic thing we can say about any human being is that we are born bearing the image of God. Like God, we love life; we are creative. Like God, we expect to find meaning in life. Like God, we love and are loved.

We believe too that nothing can change God's love for us. There is nothing we can do to make God stop loving us. Whether or not we are Christians, whether or not we have ever darkened the door of a church, God's love for us is unchanging.

Christians believe in that love. We are aware of it, and trust God's love enough to try to live in its shadow. We belong to a people with a long story. We became part of that people – initiated into the church – through the service of baptism. You might say that baptism is the Christian's way of expressing what we believe about ourselves and about God.

By pouring water on our head, the priest – on behalf of the whole church – affirms that we are part of the world of nature and united with the whole of creation. The water is the symbol of life. Baptism reminds that life itself – our life in the human family – is a gift, as surely as the water is nature's gift to us. Baptism is the church's celebration of life.

Our Watery Beginnings

At baptism, we are made part of the Christian family, just as we symbolically recall our membership in the human family. The church speaks of baptism as a new birth because when someone is baptized, that person is born into the Christian family. We are given a new identity – for the first time, we are now members of the People of God.

Of course, most of us can't even remember when we were baptized. Parents generally bring their children to church for baptism when they are still babies. We really had no choice in the matter. Certainly we didn't know what was being done for us, on our behalf. But then, we didn't have any choice in whether or not we would be born, either. Life is always a gift. People are not born because they decide to be born, nor are most Christians baptized because they decide to be born into the Christian family. If you were baptized when you had nothing to say about it, your baptism was a gift your parents gave you.

On the other hand, your parents made some specific promises in your name when you were baptized. In fact, this book is written using the questions they were asked, and the promises they made, as its outline. If you feel as if you should not be bound by promises someone else made for you, you are right. it was appropriate during your childhood that they give you a model of what kind of person they hoped you would become. Every parent has expectations of how a daughter or son will grow up. But as you approach maturity, the time comes when you must choose for yourself. Perhaps you will eventually want to make the promises expected of Christians for yourself – that is, you will want to *confirm* those vows. On the other hand, you are free to reject them. God has not trapped you into making promises you did not choose. *Confirmation* is the service in which people who were baptized before they had any say in the matter have the chance to make the promises for themselves.

But even if you decide not to follow through with the commitments which adult Christians make for themselves, you will never lose your membership in the Christian family. Baptism is forever. Once you have been born into your own family, there is nothing anyone can do to change that fact. You bear the heredity your parents gave you. You will be short or tall, your skin will be brown or black or white or red, you will be female or male. Those facts about you are given, whether you like them or not. You may leave home and go halfway around the world, you may change your name, lose touch with the people and places from your past; yet you are marked forever with the identity your parents gave you, and you will pass it on to your own descendants. In the same way, baptism gives you an eternal identity as a member of the People of God.

And just what, exactly, would it mean if you decided to accept membership in the People of God for yourself? What is it like to claim your membership?

In the first place, it means accepting what baptism tells us about who we are. It means that we belong to the world of nature – that the water in which we were created, and which still makes up the greater part of our bodies, is a clue to who and what we are. We are a part of the universe, with bonds and ties to everything that exists. This means that we have a responsibility to care for the earth and the whole of creation. But if we believe what baptism tells us, we also consider ourselves – we human beings – to be created in God's image; we owe our very life to God, and we belong to him.

Finally, at the time of our baptism, the priest marked our forehead with the sign of the cross. That is the clue to its full meaning. If we accept our baptism for ourselves, it is because we have decided that Jesus really does have the last word about what it means to be human. It means that we will plan to live as he taught us to live – not because we are afraid, but because we begin to see why his way makes more sense. Of course we know that we don't always live up to what Jesus showed us. Probably we never will. But we also see that God knows what we are like, and is willing to forgive us when we fall short of what we might be.

[15]

Being a member of the People of God gives you a history – a past full of stories, ancestors in faith, and a great deal to think about. Sooner or later, you will have to decide whether you want to take your membership seriously or not. But the choice is yours, and the option is always open. It will never be too late to claim for yourself what God has been offering you since the day you came to be.

A People and Its Story

Any human family consists of people of all ages, some of whom live nearby while others have moved across the country or the world. A family also includes those who have died and those who have not yet been born. Every family has a collection of stories, special times and places, that belong to its members alone. Those memories are told and passed on whenever families get together. Sometimes they last for many years and spread thousands of miles, as people move from place to place.

§

It was a hot August morning when Philip began putting his gear together. The most important thing was his fishing rod. It had belonged to his grandfather, and some of Philip's earliest memories were of going fishing with him. Even when he was so small he had to run to keep up, his grandfather would stop by and they would go off together. Those outings were one of the things Philip had missed most since his grandfather died. Now he was old enough to enjoy going alone, but it wasn't the same.

Philip's brother Charlie was five years younger. At nine, he was too young to remember Grandad. Sometimes Charlie stared at the photograph in the dining room, but although he tried and tried, there was no memory of him, only that picture.

For a long time, Charlie had been trying to talk his brother into taking him fishing. This morning was no different. "Come on, Phil," he began as Philip was packing his lunch for a day on the river. "Please let me come with you."

"You'll make too much noise," Philip replied, as he always did.

"No, I won't; I promise I won't make a sound."

Philip looked down at his brother, so eager for this expedition. For the first time, he decided to give it a try.

"Okay, but the first sound out of you and we're coming home, and that's the last time you'll ever get a chance!"

Their house was only a few blocks from the river. It was wide and slow, and there was a huge willow tree on the bank where Philip and his grandfather used to sit. That was the spot Phil chose for this morning's expedition.

The day passed as slowly as August days always seemed to go. Charlie was fascinated by how much Philip knew about fishing in this river. Philip showed his brother how to bait his hook, how to cast the line so that it missed the tangle of roots by the edge of the shoreline, and – when at last there was a twitching on Charlie's line – how to set the hook and reel in the fish. After they had eaten their sandwiches, they walked along the bank and Philip pointed out some of his other favorite spots. Charlie was amazed. As they walked home in the late afternoon, he asked Phil, "How did you ever learn so much about fishing?"

"That's easy," Phil answered. "Grandad taught me all about it. He knew places on that river where nobody else goes fishing, and he told me it was his father who showed them to him."

And then Philip began to talk about his grandfather: how much he had liked to be with him, what a good story-teller he was, how his grandfather used to take him on walks in the woods when the leaves were falling and build huge piles for Phil to jump in. Charlie was intrigued. He had never know this man Phil remembered, but when they got home he looked again, long and hard, at the photograph in the dining room. It seemed as if the old man was no longer a stranger. He had become almost a friend.

§

The day he went fishing with his older brother, Charlie learned something very important about being a member of his family. He had never known his grandfather; and yet, through his brother, he learned things that had come from his family's past. He learned new skills, which had been in the family a long time and now belonged to him. He learned something about where he had come from, and the people who had belonged to his family before he was born. He didn't have to go to a class to learn these things. He learned them through stories, and by watching his brother repeat what he had already learned. His brother passed on the stories about his grandfather that mattered to him, so that now, in a way, they belonged to Charlie too. From that day on, whenever Charlie would go fishing, he would remember the stories of his grandfather and what his brother had taught him. Fishing would not be just another pastime; it would be a way of remembering some of his family's most prized memories. Rosalie, their little sister, was only five now, but already Charlie could imagine himself taking her fishing some day – when she was old enough not to make too much noise and scare the fish.

§

You could say that Christians are also a family. The community of Christians is bound together by memories, by the things they have in common, by their love for one another, and by all the hopes they share which have not yet come true. Most of the time, we don't think much about what we have in common with other Christians. But there are many things we share. For one thing, we tell the same stories. If you travel five thousand miles and go to church, you will hear the same tales about Jesus and his companions that you heard at home. Christians also celebrate the same things. We all participate in holidays like Christmas and Easter. Even though one part of the family may have different customs for celebrating, the holidays are the same – just as one branch of your family may eat turkey for Christmas, and another may choose roast beef. For twenty centuries, Christians have been baptizing their children and sharing bread and wine together.

You might say, too, that Christians are members of a community. Communities also share memories and stories, share special actions and gestures. Have you ever gone to a new school? Part of learning to feel at home and *belonging* comes from hearing stories about a particular teacher or a legendary football game, picking up the slang that identifies you as a student of that school, wearing a school jacket or T-shirt. When you begin to know and understand these memories and rituals, you have become part of the community. Years later, the words of a football cheer or your school's song will remind you of what it was like to be there.

Americans feel the same way about belonging to a people. No matter what we look like, where our families came from, what race we are, whether we live in Oregon or South Carolina, we share symbols and memories of what it means to be an American. We share ancestors: Betsy Ross, George Washington, Sojourner Truth, Abraham Lincoln, Martin Luther King, and the astronauts are all part of the past we hold together. We share symbols. The flag means *The United States* wherever in the world we go. As Americans, we are part of a very large community.

§

Christians are also a people. We have ancestors we share: we are all the spiritual descendants of Abraham and Sarah. Christians trace their ancestry through the people of Israel to the time of Jesus, and then through the company of Jesus' friends who have carried on his story through two thousand years. This Christian people is the *church*.

Christians are a people who have tried for as long as they have been in existence to understand what it means to be part of this family, this community. They have wondered about God, and the universe. They have tried to figure out how human beings ought to live, what is the purpose of their lives, how to find love and what to do about the fact that we all die sooner or later. Sometimes they have tried to find ways of avoiding those questions, but the questions keep coming back.

Like any family, the church has customs and ideas with which almost all its members agree. It also has ideas which are the subject of long and loud arguments. (Any family has subjects that cause arguments whenever they come up!) Our ancestors knew less than we do about many things. They also knew more than we do about some things. But the conversations and questions and the arguments have gone on for as as long as there has been a Christian people.

We call the church's understanding about God, the world, and human life *theology*. It is a word the Greeks used to mean "the study of God." We also believe that God *wants* us to understand, and that God uses the church as a community for revealing to us what God is like – and what life is about. Theology is the way we make sense of things.

§

The People of God began with Sarah and Abraham, the first of our ancestors about whom we know anything. The people's story continues through a period of many centuries. It is recorded in the *Bible*. The Bible is the story of the people of God and what those people believed and wondered about. It is also the story of their good times and their tragedies. Above all the Bible is the story of their life with God, and how they came to know more about God. The Bible records their failures and their mistakes as well as their successes. The stories in the Bible are about real people, very much like us. Unfortunately, sometimes people seem to want to find people better or wiser or smarter than we are when they read the stories of the Bible. They try to twist them into figures who are unreal, almost inhuman – too good to be true. But if you read the Bible as the story of real-life people, you will find that they have the same problems you have. I can find my doubts and questions there, and I can also find accounts of people making the same mistakes I make. What they all have in common is their understanding that if they want to live as human beings in this world of ours, they need to know God. Real life is life with God. That is the main point of the stories in the Bible.

If you read the whole of the Bible, you will find how faith in God began in the ancient history of the human family. The earliest traces of faith go back to people who lived in tents and tended their flocks at the dawn of what we know about the human story. They understood very little about God, or about the world. But as time passed, people began to see more clearly what God was trying to show them, and they also probed more deeply into the way the world is put together. The more they learned about the world, the more they understood about God. By the time Jesus appeared, people know a great deal more than they had when the first stories found their way into the Bible.

§

Here is one of the most ancient of the Bible's stories.

Once upon a time, God looked over the whole of the earth and noticed how wicked and corrupt people had become. He was so angry that he decided to eliminate them and start over. However, there was one man who stood out from the rest because of his righteousness, a man named Noah. God decided that Noah didn't deserve to die, so he told him to build a large wooden boat, big enough to hold two of each species of creature on earth, so that life would continue. Noah obeyed God, built the boat, and loaded it with the representatives of the animals, as well as with his own family. Rain fell for forty days, until the whole world was awash. Except for the creatures in Noah's boat, everything was destroyed. When it was all over, God promised Noah that he would never again be so destructive, and as a reminder of that promise, place a rainbow in the sky.

§

Is the story of Noah true? How we answer that question depends on what we mean by it. If we mean, did God really intend to destroy most of the human race, and was there really a flood that covered the earth, and did Noah really save all the creatures from destruction, then the answer is *no*. We now know how many different kinds of animals there are on this planet of ours; we know that they fill whole zoos, and that no boat could ever hold them all. We also know more about God than the people who told the story. We now understand that God is forgiving, not given to losing his temper and changing his mind. We certainly don't believe that God needs the rainbow to remind himself not to lose his temper again! Our whole understanding of God and the world is different. We trust science to tell us about what happened in the past, and we know that the story-tellers who passed on the ancient tales in the beginning of the Bible were no scientists.

On the other hand, the story is true in what it tells us about the faith our ancestors had. For one thing, they understood that God has expectations for the human race, and that God is displeased and sad when people behave wrongly. They also understood that God cares about what happens to the world – otherwise, why would they go to such trouble to make sure all the animals made it into Noah's boat? Finally, they believed that they didn't have to fear God, and every time they saw a rainbow it served them as a reminder of their faith. In that sense, the story is true.

§

The Bible is not a book about science, or about nature. It is a story-book, the story of a people and their faith. It is the story of how God spoke to them through their faith.

We still read the Bible because it is the summary of life with God as our people lived it for many centuries. It is the heart of our story, from the time of Sarah and Abraham up through the years after Jesus. But the story is not finished. All faith keeps on growing and changing. No one believes today exactly what people believed in Jesus' time.

We are still part of the story of faith, and we are telling that story whenever we try to make sense out of God and the world. The more we know about God, and the more we know about the world, the more the story of the People of God lives on.

- - - - - -

Until a few hundred years ago, everyone thought that the earth was the center of the universe. They were certain the sun and all the planets revolved around the earth. "Experts" assured them it was true; it seemed to make sense. Now we know differently. We know that this planet of ours is a tiny speck in the vastness of space, moving around an insignificant star we call the sun, located towards the edge of our galaxy. Does that change the way we think about God? How?

Less than two hundred years ago, people were sure that God had created human beings very much as we are today, and that it had happened only a few thousand years ago. Then people began to explore ways of dating fossil remains, and they discovered the remains of ancestors hundreds of thousands, even millions, of year old. Not only have our ancestors been around much longer than we knew, it turns out that other creatures – apes, chimpanzees, gorillas – are our long-lost cousins! How did the discovery that human beings are related to other parts of the animal world change the way we think about being human? How does it change what we believe about God?

Now that we have the technology to listen to sounds from the far reaches of space, astronomers train their listening devices toward other galaxies. Many people claim to have seen UFO's, which they believe may have come from other planets. All of us are familiar with movies about visitors from space. We are getting used to the idea that there might well be intelligent life, perhaps far more advanced than ours, on other planets or in other corners of the universe. What effect does this have on the way we conceive of being human? What does it say about God?

- - - - - - -

Questions such as these never occurred to the people who told the stories which eventually found their way into the Bible. They are the questions *we* must ask and try to answer. When we do so, we are working with theology just as much as those ancient story-tellers were. We still rely on their stories to understand our past, and to help us ask the right questions for ourselves. Christians believe that the most important questions about being human are already in the Bible, and that some of the answers we find there make sense to us today – and always will.

The Mystery of God

"Where are you going, Brad?" It was his little sister's voice.

"Out." He was already late, and was in no mood for questions.

"Where are you going, Brad?" Her voice was more insistent this time.

"I said I was going out!" He slammed the door behind him to end the conversation.

The last few years had certainly been different, thanks to the presence of a child in the house. Until Alice had arrived on the scene, Brad had been the youngest. His older sister was already in college, and his brother was a senior in high school. All three had been shocked when their parents had told them the news: a baby was on the way.

It was the first time Brad had ever witnessed a pregnancy so near at hand. Watching his mother's waistline begin to grow was a strange experience. He would never forget her rapid departure in the middle of the night, or the sight of his new sister when he saw her at the hospital for the first time. His grandmother swore that Alice looked just like him, but Brad could see no resemblance at all between the face he saw in the mirror and the wrinkled, red-faced creature he observed through the glass of the hospital nursery.

It was incredible. Only the other day this infant was an invisible presence in his mother's body. Now she was a person – with a mind of her own, to judge by the volume of her crying.

The mysteries continued. The baby grew into an infant, and Brad surprised himself by discovering how delighted he was with her. The first step, the first word, astonished and excited him.

But her questions! Once she began to speak, her curiosity seemed to have no limits, and Brad was losing patience. *Where?* and *How?* and especially

Why? seemed to fascinate Alice. It was as if she wanted to know everything.

He got into the car beside his mother. "She's driving me crazy!" he exploded. "I can't even leave the room without telling her where I'm going."

"I know," his mother answered. "It does get on your nerves. But, Brad, I'll tell you something. You did the same thing when you were her age. I remember once you asked me why the clouds don't stand still. You didn't like my answer, and you kept on about it for days. It got so I was glad when the sun went down so you couldn't see the clouds for a while."

"Really?" said Brad. "I don't remember that at all. I suppose it must be odd, being new to the world."

"Yes," agreed his mother. "And you know, there are plenty of things I still don't understand. I guess you get out of the habit of asking. When I was pregnant with Alice I was reminded all over again of how mysterious life is. I mean, here is this life growing inside me, and yet it's not part of *me* at all. That life came into being just because your father and I love each other. And yet she's so different from either one of us I'll never really understand her. I wonder *why*. So I don't blame Alice for her questions. I ask them, too. I guess it's just part of being human to want to understand."

§

Life is full of mysteries. But life itself is a mystery. Look at a turtle at rest beside a rock. They look remarkably alike, yet suddenly there is a twitch and the turtle moves, while the rock remains still. We plant seeds in the ground, as people have been doing for thousands of years. They seem lifeless, yet we watch confidently for plants to sprout and grow. What curious energies pulse through the universe to call life into being?

A child is born, grows up, ages, and dies. One moment it is a living being of great complexity, the product of millions of years of evolution. The human brain alone is a miracle. It carries a lifetime of memories and information. The heart beats, the blood courses and flows, the lungs expand and contract, the human being breathes. Then in an instant the systems shut down, and what remains is a cold lifeless object as dead as if it had never been alive at all.

What a mystery is the endless cycle of life and death! Human beings have always marvelled at the wonder of being alive. And they have always been aware that life is a *gift*. It can be taken away, but never manufactured. Even if science could one day put together chemical elements in such a way that life were born, living would still be a *gift*. The scientists will not *decide* how life comes to be; they will only *discover* it. The secret is already there, waiting to be found.

The whole universe is full of such wonders. Can you imagine what it would have been like to be among the first people to set foot on the moon? Or to peer through a telescope for the first time? Or to look through a microscope at a drop of water and see what no one had known was there?

But if the universe amazes *us*, think how mysterious it must have been in ancient times. As horrible as a volcano can be, at least we understand how it comes to erupt. As terrifying as it is to live through an earthquake, we understand why it happens and can even notice warnings so that we are not always caught by surprise. The first centuries of the human story were lived without the kind of information that helps us understand the way the universe behaves. If you have ever been in the woods at night, you know how eerie and ominous the darkness can be. But suppose every night were as dark and mysterious as that! Imagine the terrors life held for our ancient ancestors, before science, before fire, before speech. The earth was full of terror; every animal was a potential predator, and every storm a fearsome nightmare.

Food was the object of a never-ending search; if the hunt was unsuccessful, people starved. No one knew anything of their neighbors; beyond their little band there were only strangers, probably dangerous strangers.

In such a world, life was a mysterious and wonderful gift. Whatever nurtured life was to be revered and honored. Deep in the caves of southern France, archaeologists have discovered magnificent paintings of animals now long extinct. The animals dance and thunder through the darkness, their bright colors undimmed by the centuries. Other archaeologists have dug up thousands of small carved female figures, many of them pregnant, the bellies rounded to emphasize their motherhood.

Surely our ancient ancestors went to the trouble to paint those animals and carve those mother-figures because life was so precious to them. They understood that nothing could be more important, or even sacred, than the energy which calls life into being and which feeds and enriches life once it has begun.

The wonder that our ancestors felt for the life-giving energy of the universe was perhaps their first experience of God. Touched and awed by its mystery, they celebrated and worshipped the power and spirit of life which they saw all around them and even sensed in themselves.

Yet nature is not only fertile and generous. Death is also part of nature – cruel and unexpected death. Lightning slashes through the dense forest and fire rages, destroying whatever lies in its path. Storms shake the heavens, winds send trees and branches flying through the air. The earth heaves and buckles, fire and smoke belch from the mountaintop. The sea, gentle and warm, becomes a monster, waves breaking in fury on the helpless coastline. To our ancestors, such moments did not simply happen. If unseen forces call life into being and feed and care for us, then surely, they reasoned, other similar forces must be in control of the fearsome aspects of nature. In their fear and awe, our ancestors assumed that divine power and anger were at work in the world, wreaking disaster where they chose. Gradually, they came to see the whole universe as populated with gods and goddesses who did as they pleased, and whose anger could bring destruction. The divine seemed to be both kind and cruel, life-giving and deadly. Behind the mystery of the universe loomed unknown deity, to be worshiped and also feared.

We can still see hints of this ancient understanding of God in the early books of the Bible. The Hebrew people preserved many tales from a time when they understood very little about God. We can still read them today. They are of interest to us, because they show us something of how faith in God began.

The Mystery of God

§

Ancient people usually believed that the divine beings who ruled the universe occupied the parts of the cosmos about which they knew the least. Since the sky seemed both near at hand and yet inaccessible, the gods who knew the most about us were often assumed to be "up there" resting on the heaven – a solid roof over our earth. Those "sky gods" were understood to be very powerful and, like great rulers on earth, extremely jealous of their rights and authority.

One day, the Hebrew people used to say, our ancestors decided to build a tower in order to climb up and reach the divine dwelling-place. They gathered and began to construct a tower which would touch heaven. The God of heaven looked down with alarm at their success and their ability. Before the tower was completed, God intervened in a very cunning way: he confused their speech, so that the people working on the tower no longer spoke the same language. Now it was impossible for them to complete the tower, since they could not communicate with each other. God's abode was safe; people would never be able to reach heaven through their own efforts.

This very old folk-tale tells us a great deal about what people once believed about God. They assumed that the existence of different languages, which caused them so much confusion, must have come about because God wanted it that way. They could not believe that things happen by accident. But even more importantly, they believed in a God who is jealous of his status and who wanted to keep people in their place. People who conceive of God in such a way must have been very uncomfortable in the universe; they must have found it a confusing and unsafe place to live, if God seemed so bent on keeping them down.

Most important of all, the tale reminds us that people have always wanted to make sense of things. Stories such as this one helped them to understand the mystery in their life.

It would be easy for us to make fun of the faith of people who understood so much less than we do. We can smile at the idea that you reach the sky by building a tower, or that heaven is a blue dome with holes for the rain to come through. Yet those images helped people to make sense of things, and to be at home in the universe. They could not understand the cosmos as we see it, nor could they understand God as we do. But they perceived a power and source of life behind the mystery, a power to which they gave the name of God. The Hebrews feared and worshiped that God, because they believed that it was God on whom they depended for their very life. Nature itself, they believed, shows us something of God. Because they assumed that the dangerous side of nature was the result of God's anger, they feared to displease him. Yet the Hebrews also worshiped God with gratitude. Despite the limitations of their understanding, they knew that life itself is God's gift, and that whatever feeds and strengthens us is from God. "God," they told each other, "is like a shepherd, guarding and protecting those in his charge."

Here is an ancient Hebrew poem which makes that point:

The Lord is my shepherd; I shall not want.

He makes me lie down in green pastures;
he leads me beside strengthening, refreshing streams.

He restores my life; he leads me on the right road, to honor his name.

Yes, even if I should walk through the valley of the shadow of death, I will fear no evil, for you are with me; your crook and staff support me.

You prepare a table for me in the presence of my enemies; you anoint my head with oil; my cup overflows.

Surely goodness and mercy will follow me all the days of my life; and I will live in the Lord's house forever. *(Psalm 23)*

- - - - - - -

This poem was written about three thousand years ago. How would you describe the poet's understanding of God?

What would you agree with in the poet's view of God? What seems old-fashioned or outdated?

- - - - - - -

Whenever people try to think about God, they form pictures in their mind of what God must be like. Our ancient ancestors probably thought of God as a mother, bringing forth life, or as a father, providing for his children. In those times, the world of *nature* was the setting for faith. Most of what happened to people was the result of natural forces. There were no nations; there was no history.

The story of civilization describes how people gradually learned to settle down, to plant crops and then remain to harvest them. Animals were tamed and put to human service. The land, which had been free for the using, became a possession; people learned to defend the places they had settled. They formed tribes, built villages and towns, chose chiefs and even kings. Jericho, the first city, dates from about ten thousand years ago. Its ruins survive only a short distance from Jerusalem.

Once people had learned to live in cities, the world changed dramatically. It had taken human beings millions of years to arrive at the knowledge and skill they needed to live in towns. Once they did so, history was born. Within a few thousand years the earth was divided up into great empires. Egypt, China, India, and the Middle East all provided settings for the growth of human ability – and human power.

Now the setting of human life had changed. Before, it was the natural cycle of birth and death, and the accidents of nature, that determined what a person's life would be like; now, it was history. Of course the power of nature remained, but the important forces and events that made things happen took place in history. Now people had to fear not only earthquake and windstorm, but the great marauding armies of their enemies. Like a swarm of locusts, giant forces of soldiers appeared on the horizon, their origin unknown, riding furiously in the hot sun, swords flashing, dealing destruction wherever they went. One after the other, the great empires swept with their armies over the earth: the Pharaohs of Egypt, the Assyrians, Alexander the Great, the Romans.

Wherever they went people's lives were drastically changed. Death was as likely to come from human violence as from a natural disaster. Famine might occur because the rains never came, but it might also be the result of an invasion by troops who burned the fields and slaughtered the farmers.

People first worshiped God in the hope that nature would be kind to them, and in gratitude for the gift of life. Now they also worshiped the God they hoped could save them from their enemies, and whose power would be able to turn aside those foreign gods to whom their enemies prayed.

Our ancestors in faith, the Hebrew people, suffered more from their slavery in Egypt than they had ever experienced at the hands of nature alone. The God to whom they prayed was the God who could help them escape from their slavery. When Moses, their great leader, brought them out of Egypt and led them through the desert towards the land they called home, they were certain that their God was responsible for their rescue.

The Book of Exodus describes how Moses begged Pharaoh, the ruler of Egypt, to allow the Hebrews to leave Egypt peacefully. He refused, since he relied on their slave-labor to help in his royal construction projects. Moses warned him that God would punish Egypt if the Hebrews were not allowed to go, but

Pharaoh continued to insist that they could not leave. Then, the story tells us, a series of disasters began to occur, among them plagues of lice, locusts, frogs, flies, and a mysterious red-colored pollution of the Nile River, which killed fish and crops alike. We might consider these natural disasters, but the story-teller was convinced they were no accident. He believed that God was fighting on the Hebrews' behalf. Finally, the worst disaster of all struck the Egyptians: the Pharaoh's own son died, and with him, so the story goes, the first-born son of every Egyptian family. Even their livestock was stricken. At last Pharaoh was convinced, and Moses hastily led the people away by night, without even waiting for their bread to rise before they baked it. (When their descendants commemorate this escape, they recall the flight from Egypt by eating unleavened bread, or *matzoh*. This is the Jewish holiday of *Passover*.)

Even though he had given permission for the Hebrews to leave, Pharaoh soon changed his mind and sent an army to capture them. But at the Sea of Reeds (which the story-tellers mistook for the Red Sea) the people were able to safely cross the marshy ground with the army almost upon them. While the Egyptians' chariots were trying to follow, the tide came in and the army was drowned. The oldest piece of literature in the Bible comes from the victory celebration of the Hebrews, which the prophetess Miriam sang through the night as the women danced on the shore:

Sing to the Lord, for he has triumphed gloriously!
The horse and the rider he has thrown into the sea.

- - - - - - -

What do you think of the God whom the
Hebrews worshipped by the seashore? How
is this image different from the poem that
calls the Lord a *shepherd*?

- - - - - - -

Once they had been set free from their slavery, the
Hebrew people continued to believe that God was in
control of nature, but now they also believed in God
as the ruler of history. They were certain that God
had plans for them, plans that would include the way
they lived as a nation. The Hebrews considered
themselves God's chosen people, selected from
among all the peoples of the earth to do God's will.
They believed that God had set them free for a
purpose, and that they had come to know God in a
special way. The Bible describes this as a *covenant*
– a set of promises in which each party pledges faithfulness to the other. The Hebrew people promised to
keep God's demands to worship only *this* God, who
had brought them out of slavery; to revere God's
name, and not to implicate him in falsehood by using
his name to swear to a lie; to keep one day out of

seven as a day of honor to God, by doing no work; and to promise never to construct an image of God, since the reality of God is beyond any living thing we could imagine. God also commanded the Hebrews to honor their parents, and forbade murder, stealing, lying and envy. Husbands and wives must pledge faithfulness to each other.

In return for their obedience, the Hebrews could count on God to remain faithful to his special bond with them, and to nurture them as a people of justice and peace. This law, the Ten Commandments, was meant to be the way by which the Hebrew people could honor God in their own lives by living rightly with others. The God of the Hebrews was now seen to be the Lord of history; whatever happened to them, they believed that God was with them, protecting them if they would only keep their part of the covenant, fighting on their side, and bringing prosperity and plenty in return for faithfulness.

- - - - - - -

How would you expect the Hebrews' lives to have changed by keeping these Ten Commandments? What would their practical effect have been?

- - - - - - -

What a long story is the story of faith! How much more about God the Hebrew people understood than the people who lived before them. They were growing up. God, they had come to believe, is not bound to nature, but can be seen in events that changed the course of history. If we look back on their images of God, we will probably find them inadequate in some ways for us, just as they found inadequate the beliefs of those who lived long before them. Yet they made discoveries that changed forever the way we understand God. These discoveries help us to make better sense of life.

God is constantly waiting for us to be able to see clearly. As the human family tries to know God more fully, God is forever revealing more and more about himself. As soon as we reach a point where still more truth would make sense to us, God shows us that much more about what he is like. By the time the Hebrews escaped from their slavery, they had already come to know a great deal about God. But the story was not over, not by a long way. There was still far more about God waiting to be discovered and understood.

For that matter, we have still not reached the end of the story. No doubt there are amazing truths about God that we are still not capable of grasping, just as we still don't understand the mysteries of life and death. But God is waiting for us to be ready to see more clearly. God still leads us to new and deeper truth. There are mysteries we haven't even thought of. But God will be there when we are ready.

Finding the Mystery

It was Susan's fifth-grade teacher who made it possible for her to go to camp. It was the first time Susan had ever been in the country. Once in a while, her mother took her to the park, but after the woman in the upstairs apartment was knocked down and robbed just inside the park gates, her mother decided it was too dangerous. So when Susan's teacher offered her the chance to spend two weeks at camp, it was like a dream.

Years later, she could still remember the first day – she had gotten sick on the bus just before they arrived at the camp. That night she could hardly sleep because it was so quiet, and yet the night was alive with creatures she had never heard before. How strange that trains and shouts and breaking glass were almost more comfortable for her than the sounds of the country – her counselor told her it was just the wind in the trees, or a cricket, or perhaps a raccoon. After that night, though, everything seemed wonderful. Susan had cried when the last day came and she had to get on the bus for the long ride back to the city.

The next year, Susan's mother couldn't afford even the small amount of money that was needed for camp. Since that summer, Susan had hardly ever been outside the city, and she had never again heard the night noises, or smelled the fresh air after the storms, or run across the fields just for the fun of it. There was no place to run in her neighborhood except down sidewalks where people sat for hours in the hot sun, telling stories and playing dominoes. No one seemed to have anything else to do.

Susan belonged to a girls' club that met in the basement of an old, unused school. When she was younger, she had gone to the school, and could remember playing in the yard out back. Now the school was closed, and the dirt in the playground was packed so hard it was impossible to imagine anything growing there. Broken bottles were everywhere and her mother had warned her to stay out, especially when it was getting dark.

One day as she was going into the school for a club

meeting, Susan had an idea. She thought about it for a moment, then burst into the room where most of the members were already waiting. "Listen!" she began. "I just had an idea! Suppose we turned that old playground into a garden." "A garden!" her friend Mary Beth said. "You must be kidding! Who's going to plant a garden? Who's going to take care of it? You know the kids would tear it up as soon as we got it finished. And besides, people would steal from it if anything did grow – which I doubt."

Several other people agreed, but Teresa, a volunteer who helped with the girls' club, agreed with Susan. "It's worth a try," she said. "Maybe some of your parents would give us a hand, and if we got enough people from the neighborhood to help out, they might even be able to keep it safe. If you'd like, we could speak to someone from the Board of Education and see what happens."

A few weeks later the digging began. Susan wouldn't have believed it if she hadn't seen it. The first morning, there were seven people on hand digging up the playground. By lunchtime, most of them were tired and had gone home, but ten others had taken over. By the time they finished for the day, more than half the playground had been dug up.

Once people saw that there really was going to be a garden, they came to watch, and sooner or later most of them did some work as well. By July, the playground was a tiny version of what Susan remembered from the country. Her mother had a row of vegetables, and even a few ears of corn. No one was sure if the corn would grow, but it did. In Susan's row, there were only flowers. "I don't want to grow food," she told her mother. "I want to see some real, bright red flowers in that park." Her mother came home with four packets of seeds, and Susan planted them just as the directions said. The carnations died, but the rest came up and one day, there was a bud on one of the zinnias. Soon there were flowers growing along the whole length of Susan's row.

Summer passed, fall came, and school started. Gradually the garden took on a winter look; plants turned brown and died. The flowers wilted and then it snowed, and Susan's garden was gone for another year. But there was no question about next spring. There would be a garden. Susan would see to that.

§

There is something very *creative* about gardening. It means taking a piece of ground that is barren or overgrown with weeds and turning it into a place of growing things. It is the gardener who decides what is to grow where. You could even say that a gardener is something of an artist, bringing beauty out of the everyday.

There is a special joy which comes from being creative. You know this if you have ever baked a perfect loaf of bread, or painted a picture you love, or spent many hours building a model ship or car. Every human being has such an impulse. We like to bring something out of nothing, and to produce things which give pleasure. The most creative act of all is bringing new life into being. That is how the human species, and every species, reproduces itself.

When we are being creative, we are most like God who, after all, has been bringing things into being for a long time. No wonder our ancestors told stories about God as a gardener! They were trying to say that God is a *creative* God.

All of nature reflects creativity in some way. Spiders weave astonishing patterns into their webs. Every snowflake is a marvel of geometry. Birds behave like builders when they construct their nests, and sing melodies as fine as any music. But nature is creative by instinct. Birds don't design their nests; they simply build them the way they have always been built.

Human creativity is different. We human beings *decide* how to be creative. We move colors around, we play with words, and we turn the objects of our attention this way and that. We are conscious artists, choosing what to do and how to do it. That sets us apart from other creatures, and makes us like God.

[53]

We are different from the rest of creation in another way as well. I doubt very much if a porcupine asks why it looks the way it does, or if a crocodile ever contemplates flying. But we human beings have imaginations; we can think of alternatives. We can wonder why people act the way they do. Although all creatures die, *we* can ask ourselves why that should be true – in other words, we can imagine what it would be like if things were different.

If there is such a thing as a meaning to our life, it would have to be something so basic that everyone could understand and share it; otherwise, it might give meaning to some people, but not to everyone.

The reason we Christians take Jesus so seriously is that he identified what might indeed turn out to give meaning to life. It is something we all can understand, and we all can share. Jesus claimed that what gives life meaning is *love*.

It was Jesus' vision of the possibility of loving and of being loved that gave his own life meaning. Who among the whole human race would not wish for love? Who would want to go through life without ever knowing what it means to be cared for?

But love is something more that we share with God. It is God who loved us first, loved us into existence and who loves us for all eternity. No human being could love us like that, even if we might wish it could be true. Only God could love us that much. Everything that exists in the universe, we believe, has come into being because of God's love. Yet it is the human family that shares God's love most fully, because it is human beings who, like God, can choose how to act with one another. Animals behave towards other animals through instinct, as you know if you have ever tried to get your cat to stop killing birds. But we act as we choose, because we are free in the way God is free: free to love. We are free to care for one another.

Perhaps it is fair to say that nothing matters more to us human beings than creativity, meaning and love. These also matter to God. It is as if God were reflected in the way we seek to create, the way we find meaning, the way we love each other.

- - - - - - -

How is God like a gardener? How is God like an artist? Can you recall any moments when love has given special meaning to your life?

- - - - - - -

Our ancestors used to say that we human beings are created in God's image. In the beginning, they

[55]

took that thought literally and assumed that we *look* like God. They believed that God possessed a body not so different from a human body.

Although we no longer believe that God has a body, we still speak as if we thought it were true. For example, when we want to talk about God's power, we speak of God's hand or arm. (Remember the old song, "He's Got the Whole World in His Hands?")

Another way we still speak as if God had a body is our habit of calling God "he." The custom of speaking of God in masculine language goes back to ancient times, when our ancestors were used to a world where men held more power than women. Since they conceived of God as the ultimate power in the universe, it is not surprising that they assumed God had male characteristics. Whenever people tried to imagine what God was like, they almost always depicted "him" as male – usually an old man on a throne.

Jesus tried to help people understand that such talk about God is only symbolic. *All* human beings, male and female, share traits which belong to God. Jesus saw that God encompasses the best of what is male and female. When he wanted to convey truths about God, he used images of both men and women. For example, Jesus wanted his followers to understand that God welcomes back those who have been separated from God. He told several stories to make his point. In one of them, he compared God to a father celebrating the return of his lost son; in another, he described God as a woman looking for a coin that had been lost. In other words, if we speak of God as "he," we could just as easily speak of God as "she." If we are used to praying to God as "Our Father," we should also be able to pray to God as "Our Mother." Both kinds of language can tell us something worth knowing about God.

- - - - - - -

How would it change your understanding of God to pray to God as "Our Mother"?

- - - - - - -

We now know that God doesn't have a body at all. But that doesn't mean our ancestors were entirely wrong when they said we were created in God's image. We *do* look like God. If you search deeply enough in your own heart, you will discover that you are a creator – whether you like to write poetry or cook spaghetti. God is also a creator. You seek meaning to your life. It is God who has created life to be meaningful. You are capable of loving, and of being loved. Love is God's own heart. These facts of human life are God's image, planted and rooted in each of us. And that is no accident.

Finding the Mystery

But if in fact we do carry these reflections of God within us, it means that we possess some very important clues to understanding the mystery of God. And not only that, the clues lie within *us*. If we want to discover what God is really like, we can look into ourselves and find out. If we are created in God's image, then the more we know ourselves, the more we will know God.

That God still remains a mystery, just as your own heart contains dark secrets and can still prove to be full of surprises. But God is a mystery who keeps trying to help us know him better.

Introducing Jesus

When the Nazis were at the height of their power during the early years of the Second World War, they controlled many other countries in Europe besides their own native Germany. The Nazis could never have kept control of their conquered territory without the help of persons who cared so little about their own people that they were willing to go to work for the conquerors. Maybe they were greedy, or held a grudge against their own country; perhaps they even believed in what the Nazis taught. But whatever the reason, they earned their own country's hatred by daring to act as agents for the tyrants who had overrun their homeland.

Two thousand years ago, Israel was occupied by

the armies of the Roman Empire – one of the most powerful in the world. Rome controlled Europe all the way to the Atlantic Ocean, and as far north as England. Roman soldiers patrolled the Middle East, and grew rich from the treasures of western Asia and northern Africa. Even Egypt, the ancient kingdom where Israel had once lived in slavery, was a province of Rome. Jesus' people, the Jews, were terrorized by a cruel tyranny. Like all empires, Rome engaged the services of a few of the conquered people to do their work for them – work like collecting taxes to be sent off to Rome to make the Empire and its rulers still richer. This is a story about one such person.

§

His name was Levi. He had no friends, and had always thought of himself as an outsider. When he was growing up, for some reason people always seemed to laugh at him. Levi laughed, too, but only when others were watching. Inside, he felt ridiculous and he clenched his fists when he remembered how they had insulted him. His life was miserable, and growing up did nothing to take away his anger. It is not that he wasn't bright; but no one seemed able to get close to him. It was as if it was impossible to reach behind the mask with which Levi hid his hurt.

The tax-collector's job was perfect for him. Of course, he knew that everyone would hate him; but he told himself that it didn't matter. No one liked him anyway. Now at least they would have a reason for their hatred. And if he did his job thoroughly he would be rich: a kind of revenge for all he had suffered.

Levi proved to be right. He did get rich, and he was hated still more. He felt the stares as he walked swiftly through the market; sometimes children even threw rocks and ran away. He was more alone than ever. Of course he did not dare to go near the synagogue, where everyone gathered for prayers. Levi was the enemy of Israel, his own people; he must be the enemy of their God, his own God.

He didn't even hear of Jesus until long after everyone was talking about him. Levi was a stranger to the crowds who wondered aloud if Jesus might be the one they had been waiting for. Religion bored Levi. He assumed it had nothing to do with him.

However, one morning Levi overheard a piece of news. Jesus would be passing through town that very day. Both curious and bitter, he decided to make a point of standing at the door of the house where he collected taxes, so that he could have a look at this Jesus.

He could hear the crowd as it approached, long before he could make out any faces. When it appeared Levi wanted to run – but he stood firm. "I'm not going to hide," he told himself, "I'm not ashamed." But his breath caught when Jesus stopped by his door. The crowd gaped when they saw what was happening, and then strained to hear their talk.

"Levi," said Jesus.

"Yes," he answered, his voice wavering.

"Levi, I want you to come with me."

Now the crowd was deathly silent. They waited. Jesus nodded. Levi turned to pull the door closed behind him. They set off down the street together, to the surprise and outrage of many people in the crowd.

Levi never collected taxes for the Romans again. He became one of the Twelve, the closest of Jesus' friends who traveled with him to the city of Jerusalem where Jesus met his death. Levi's whole life was changed by the meeting with Jesus. He didn't forget the bitterness of the lonely years that had gone before; but it no longer mattered. For the first time, he knew that someone had seen *him* – as he really was, as he wanted to be, not as they made him in order to laugh at him or to hate him.

- - - - - - -

What would it be like to be Levi before he met Jesus?

Have you ever felt like Levi? What did you do about it?

What do you think Jesus noticed about him that other people had overlooked?

Why would Jesus choose someone like Levi to be with him?

- - - - - - -

All over Israel, people had the same kind of meetings with Jesus that Levi had. Jesus encountered people who had been carrying guilt for sins long past, sometimes a burden of guilt so heavy that their bodies were twisted or paralyzed. He met people with dread diseases, whose friends ran away from them; people who acted so strangely that they lived on the edge of the human family; people who were bored, afraid or lonely. All of these people discovered that when they met Jesus, things changed. They themselves seemed different. The same discovery has happened to people ever since. Jesus seems to *matter*. Most people can't imagine anyone quite like him. We use him as a comparison when we want to describe

[63]

someone particularly special. The greatest thing we can say of someone is to describe that person as *Christlike*. Sometimes people describe Mother Theresa, or Gandhi, or St. Francis, as being "like Jesus." What finer compliment could anyone pay them? In fact, Christians consider Jesus as the turning point in history, the most important person who ever lived. We count time either "B.C." – before Christ – or "A.D." – in the year of the Lord.

When you think about how significant Jesus is, it is hard to realize how little we know about his life. No one took movies of him, or recorded his voice; in fact, no one even wrote down anything about him until some years after his death. Two thousand years ago, writing was an art and books a luxury of the rich. Ordinary people learned how to read only in order to worship and to keep track of their business. On the other hand, people seem to have been much better at telling stories – and remembering them – than we are.

It is a good thing that is true, because all we know about Jesus comes from stories passed on by word of mouth. We know more about his last week than all the rest of his life. That week began with his arrival in Jerusalem to celebrate the Passover holiday in the spring in about the year 30 A.D. A few days later he was arrested and put to death.

§

But people remembered Jesus. They told and retold stories about him. Gradually, over the years, those stories were written down. By that time, people's memories had begun to get rusty, and many of those who had known him were either dead or very old. So people who were followers of Jesus' way were anxious to hold on to the stories. When the accounts of his life and death were put on paper, Christians guarded them carefully.

Four accounts of Jesus' life survive today. All were written many years later – not in the Aramaic language that Jesus spoke, but in the language spoken by ordinary people all over the Roman Empire, a form of Greek. Even Jesus' own name was translated. Mary and Joseph called him "Yeshua," which is similar to the English name, Joshua. But in Greek Yeshua became *Iesous*, and in Latin, the Empire's official language, it was *Jesus*.

Each of the four books about Jesus is slightly different. That should not surprise us. What seemed important to one writer might be left out by another; each had heard stories the others had missed; besides, each of the writers had his own point of view about Jesus. We know very little about them except their names – Matthew and Mark, Luke and John. Those four men probably did not know Jesus personally. What they had in common was their wish to help others to know about Jesus, and their belief that he

was the most important person who had ever lived –
or who would ever live. That is why their short books
about him are called "gospels," or "good news."

- - - - - -

**If you were setting out to write the story
of Jesus, what things about him would seem
most important to pass on?**

- - - - - - -

We don't know some of the things about Jesus' life
we wish we knew. His childhood and adolescent years
are almost entirely unknown. All we can assume is that
his was the life of any Jewish boy living in a little town
in Israel during the Roman occupation. His followers
weren't really interested in the kind of information we
might put into a biography. They cared more about
stories that would demonstrate the kind of man Jesus
was.

For example, one of the most remarkable things
about Jesus was that he always seemed to notice
people that no one cared about: beggars, people who
were hopelessly handicapped, the poorest of the
poor, small children. Not only did Jesus notice them,
he did remarkable things for them. Many who
thought they would always be crippled or deaf or ill
discovered that Jesus could heal them. A great part of

his fame came from his reputation as a healer.

In Jesus' day, people understood nothing about disease except its effects. The world was full of crippled and deformed people for whom there was neither hope nor cure. But Jesus cured them; no one understood how, but they assumed it must have been by God's own power.

§

One day Jesus was talking to a huge crowd. The house in which he was staying was filled with people, and others were crowded around the door.

Four men who had already heard of Jesus went to bring their crippled friend to him in the hope that Jesus would heal his suffering. When they got to the house, the men saw that there was no way they could get close enough to Jesus even to catch his eye. Still determined, they climbed to the simple tiled roof of the house and began to break open a hole. When the opening was large enough, they lowered their friend through it on a blanket until he was lying before Jesus. Jesus saw his twisted legs and was struck by his misery. He seemed to know what had crippled this man, and without a moment's hesitation, Jesus spoke to him.

"Your sins are forgiven," he said.

Immediately there was whispering in the crowd. It came from some of the other rabbis who had come to listen to their fellow teacher. "What a thing to say!" they murmured. "Who but God can forgive anyone's sins?"

Jesus heard them. He knew that it was important for everyone to understand what had happened. "You must know that I can forgive people their sins." To the man still lying in front of him, he said, "Get up! Pick up your blanket and walk home." The man, freed from the agony which had twisted his body for so long, jumped to his feet. The crowd was astonished. As for the man who had been crippled, it seemed to him as if his old life had ended and a new life had just begun.

§

Jesus was also known as a great story-teller. He taught a good deal, mostly through stories, or *parables* in which he often surprised people with what he had come to understand about God.

God, Jesus said, is not a cruel dictator or a playful trickster who uses the world as a toy. God has dreams for us – dreams which Jesus' own people had imagined for a long time. But God does not impose those dreams. God is like a loving father who cares about what happens to his children, but who also gives them the freedom they need. Jesus called God "Abba" – the Aramaic word that Jewish children used for their own fathers. God, said Jesus, is just as forgiving as any human father; we can trust God to accept us just as we are, even though God knows we can change and hopes that we will not be stuck forever the way we are.

§

The stories people remembered about Jesus were tales about life – real-life people and what happened to them when they met Jesus. They are stories about growing and changing. They are about people set free from pain, from guilt, from mistakes they wished had never happened. If you read these stories you will see in Jesus a man who was truly *creative*. Jesus saw possibilities where others noticed only victims or outcasts. It seems as if there were no dead ends for him. He never wrote anyone off; he believed there was hope for everyone. Just as God's creative energy called life into being, Jesus' creative spirit called people to come to life – people like Levi the tax-collector, or like the cripple who found he was forgiven and could walk again. The gift Jesus gave his followers was the gift of *life*, richly and fully lived.

He gave them other gifts, too, and one was the gift of love. Jesus not only noticed people, he cared for them. He was never content to pass them by; there was no doubt about how he behaved towards the people who crossed his path. Not that Jesus didn't get tired; he did. Or that he wasn't tempted to use his fame for his own sake; he was. But Jesus chose a different path. He chose to give people what they needed – attention, acceptance and dignity. Jesus wasn't forced to behave in this way. Every time he met someone, he was free to turn his back and walk away. Yet he never did. Jesus' friends had never met anyone with such care and respect for the people he saw and spoke with. He took them seriously; he gave them respect, which is the best kind of love.

§

Frances was fifteen when her brother was killed in a motorcycle accident. The night before he died, she had a date with Evan, her boy friend. After a movie, they had sat on the wall of a vacant lot down the street from her house. It was that night that Evan told her he loved her more than he had ever loved any other girl. Frances had a hard time going to sleep. Evan loved her!

And then came the next morning, the terrible morning she would never forget. Her brother, two years older, left home early and rode his motorcycle to school. It was over in an instant. The car speeded up to make it through the yellow light. Minutes later, the police were at the front door, breaking the news. A little while later and Frances would have been on the school bus, and would have missed them.

Evan heard about the accident at lunchtime. He felt sick, as he remembered that he had never really liked Frances' brother. He wondered how she must feel. Evan wondered what he could possibly say to her. How could he pretend to be sorry, when she knew he didn't like her brother anyway? What if she cried? He supposed she would. Better to wait a while, to think of something right or clever to say.

But Evan never did think of anything to say. He avoided Frances' house, and didn't call her.

Frances couldn't believe it. Only the night before, Evan had told her he loved her more than anyone. Why didn't he stop by, or at least call? It would have been so good to see him, to hear his voice. Had he somehow missed the news? That was impossible. It had been on the radio all day; everyone at school was talking about it. Night came, the worst night of her life, as she and her parents cried together as if their hearts were broken.

Evan never called. He could never think of anything to say.

§

Evan said he *loved* Frances. He probably thought he meant what he said. But did he really love her? Not if loving means choosing to care for another person. If Evan really cared for her, wouldn't he have put her above his own feelings?

Jesus, on the other hand, knew that love is not really a feeling at all, but a way of living. It is *how you act*, not how fast your heart beats. The amazing thing about Jesus is the way he chose to act towards people whom no one else even noticed or loved.

Many people cannot understand why Jesus lived as he did, but Jesus understood that it is life lived in this way that gives meaning to existence. If he had asked the people he saw around him what they were living for, most of them probably would have found it hard to answer. The soldiers marching down the road from town, hate glaring from their eyes, striking fear into the people they passed – what was their life for? Or the crowds who came looking for a miracle when Jesus came to town – did their life have a meaning? Even the powerful people in Jersualem who feared Jesus and wanted him out of the way – what were they living for? But Jesus knew what life was about. His life had meaning because it was a life of perfect love. That was what Jesus was *for*.

How do we know that Jesus understood the

meaning of his life? There is one test which anyone can use to measure what you are living for. It's the answer to the question, *What will you die for?*

Some people would die to save their families. There are many stories of parents who have given their lives to rescue their children. Others are willing to die for their country. Thousands, even millions of people have been killed because they were convinced their country deserved their sacrifice.

But what did Jesus die for? Not his family, not his friends or his own people. Jesus died as a sign of *love* – a love for all people, including those who killed him. Jesus was executed by one of the most cruel forms of death ever invented – he was nailed to a cross. Crucifixion, as this form of death is called, was the punishment the Romans saved only for political prisoners. They believed Jesus was a threat to the security of their Empire.

It might seem strange that a man willing to give his life out of love should have been considered a political threat by anyone. To understand it, we have to remember that Jesus belonged to a people who believed that God had very firm ideas about how the human family should live together. They believed that God intended for this earth to be a place of justice, harmony, abundance and compassion. If the world were put together as God meant it to be, there would be no more misery or violence, no war or hunger or cruel inequality. Some of the Jewish prophets wrote at length about what the earth would be like if God's will actually came to pass. They called that vision the "kingdom of God", because it would be a place in which God's rules are obeyed: a kingdom of peace and plenty.

But the Jews did not just try to imagine what such a world would be like as a kind of fantasy, the way we sometimes ask ourselves, "What if?" They firmly believed that some day, God would bring that world to pass. They even had a name for the person who would make it all happen. They called him "the Anointed One" – the one whom God had chosen as the founder of God's own kingdom. In Hebrew, the word for "anointed" is *Messiah*; in Greek, it is *Christos*.

Some of the Jews in Jesus' time were most interested in how God's plans would affect the Jewish people. They dreamed of a Messiah who would throw off the heavy burden of their oppression by the Romans, and make of Israel a great nation – the greatest of nations. That was why they greeted Jesus with such excitement when he arrived in Jersualem, throwing palm branches in his way as we might throw ticker-tape or confetti in a Wall Street parade.

It was certainly true that Jesus shared the dream of

the kingdom of God. When he began to travel among his people, teaching and healing, he often told them, "God's kingdom is near at hand." So when he fed the crowd, they recalled that in God's kingdom there is plenty for everyone. When he healed the sick, and embraced the lonely and the forgotten, they remembered that God's kingdom is built on kindness and love. When he spoke out against those who mistreated or cheated the poor, they called to mind the promise that in God's kingdom there is perfect justice.

So it is no wonder that Jesus made the Romans nervous. He attracted large, excited crowds, and crowds always alarmed the Romans. Even the religious leaders of Jesus' own people, the Jews, were afraid. They did not believe Jesus could do anything to help, and if he provoked the Romans they would be in worse trouble than before.

Jesus was arrested, tried before the Roman governor, Pontius Pilate, and sentenced to death – because he believed in love and lived it fully, because he dreamed of God's kingdom and longed to help it come true. Even as he hung dying on his cross, he exclaimed, "Father, forgive them! They don't know what they are doing."

§

Jesus died alone, convinced that he had been abandoned. His body was claimed by a wealthy man who was a secret admirer of Jesus and who happened to own a newly-prepared grave. Jesus' body was laid in that tomb. Like most burial places for those who could afford it, the tomb was built into a hillside and had a large stone which rolled over the opening to cover the entrance.

Jews were not allowed by their law to tend to the burial of the dead on Saturday, the Jewish day of rest. In order to honor God, all work – even the work of burial – was forbidden on the Sabbath. So it was not until Sunday morning that some of his friends made their way to the tomb with the spices normally used to prepare a body for its burial.

Dawn found several women making their way cautiously to the place where Jesus was buried, wondering who would roll away the stone for them. Much to their surprise, the tomb was open – and empty. Strangers were nearby, who told them that Jesus was not there. He had been raised from the dead.

§

Christians still celebrate that Sunday morning. We call it Easter, and we believe it changed everything.

Many people find the story of Easter almost impossible to believe. No one else had ever been raised from the dead. It was just as hard for Jesus' friends to believe; they had never heard of anyone being raised from death, either! At first, the others refused to take the women seriously when they heard their story. But then they themselves encountered Jesus again. Most of them recognized him at once; for others, it took longer, because they could not imagine it could be true. But at last they all were certain. The word spread, and years later the four writers who retold the story of Jesus wrote it all down so that the memories would never be forgotten.

§

People had always asked themselves who Jesus might be. They remembered the prophets from the past – Isaiah, Amos, Jeremiah – who had reminded Israel of its special ties to God. At first, many thought Jesus might be yet another prophet, speaking out in God's name for justice and love.

But they also remembered the belief that God would one day give them a perfect kingdom, and all that Jesus had said and done to help fulfill that hope. They thought he was the Messiah, but then he was killed. No one expected that God's "anointed one" would have to die.

When Jesus was raised from the dead, his friends were sure that he must be the Christ. If Jesus had died and was alive again, it could only be because God had raised him. No other power in the universe could do such a thing. Easter morning was the sign that what Jesus stood for – what he had lived and died for – was what God stood for. In Jesus, God's kingdom had begun.

§

Gradually people began to wonder if it was enough to say that Jesus was the Messiah. It was true as far as it went; but as they looked back on the way he lived and died, it seemed as if there must be more to it than that.

After all, think of the way he lived. He forgave people's sins; they knew they were forgiven. He spoke words of healing; pain disappeared. Wherever he went, blind people could see, lonely people found friends, and all sorts of people found their life changed. It's true, Jesus is like us – like us, he bears God's image, full of life and love and meaning. But in Jesus, the image is clear. In us, it is always confused by our own selfishness, or by the mistakes we make. In Jesus, we see that image clearly. Jesus is surely human, as human as we are. Yet he is just like God – loving, creative, understanding and forgiving. Tentatively at first and then with more confidence, his followers dared to tell the whole truth about Jesus. In this man, God is alive as fully as God could be in a human life. All the power of God's love has come to work through Jesus. When Jesus said, "Your sins are forgiven," God was acting through him. When Jesus died alone and forsaken, God was hanging on the cross. When Jesus was raised from the dead, it was God's power making itself visible. Because Jesus is who he is, his friends finally understood the whole truth about him. In Jesus, God came to live among us.

PART TWO

Will you continue in the apostles' teaching and fellowship, in the breaking of bread, and in the prayers?

I will, with God's help.

The Bread of Life

The warm moist air of a spring night cast a heavy, oppressive air over the city, adding to the tension that electrified the atmosphere. Passover was always like this: crowds of people celebrating a festival of freedom when their homeland was in slavery. No wonder they were sullen, irritable and ready to fight.

Passover is the yearly remembrance of that night when Moses led the people of Israel from the nightmare of slavery in Egypt to the land that was theirs by promise. "Why is this night different from all other nights?" asks the youngest child as the Passover ritual begins. It was the year's greatest feast, because it was the celebration of the freedom God willed for his people.

For centuries, every Jew had been glad to celebrate this holiday. But disaster followed disaster. At last the Roman Empire sent its legions to conquer them, and imposed a bitter regime which sapped their morale and carried off their resources. The soldiers who enforced Rome's rule were mindlessly cruel. Probably they never even wondered why the Jewish people saw them as their enemy. They could not afford to let down their guard even enough to ask why the Jews cared so much about being free. All they knew was that the situation was ugly and hostile, and most of all when the Jews remembered what might have been.

And Passover was a time for remembering. It was celebrated with a feast, because God had promised Israel a land of plenty – "a land flowing with milk and honey," as one poet had described it. The promise of food and drink for all must have sounded like a dream to the Hebrew people when they were slaves in Egypt, but they never lost their dream. They believed that it was God's will for them to eat their fill in a land of freedom. Whatever the hunger and thirst of the present, they believed that one day they would never be hungry or thirsty again. This was their dream of the kingdom of God.

The Jews believed their dream would come true because they trusted God to make it happen. But years came and went, and the kingdom of God seemed as far off as ever. Yet they kept waiting and hoping, mostly because they still remembered how God had once brought them into freedom. Passover for the Jews in Jersualem in Jesus' day was a bitter-sweet season. It was a time for remembering the promise and the freedom that had once been theirs, and for wondering when it would be true for them again. But even as the Roman troops tried to remind people of how overwhelming was the might of the Roman Empire, the Jewish people feasted, in memory and in hope.

On the night that Passover began, Jesus and his friends made their way, hidden by darkness, to an upstairs room where secret plans had been laid for them to eat the meal. Jesus was the center of every-one's attention. Only a few days earlier, he had ridden into Jerusalem on a donkey; he knew that if he did this people would claim him as their king. He had decided that the time had come when they should have the opportunity to hear what he had to say: God has drawn near. God's kingdom is at hand. Those in power had better beware and recognize that God's love is more powerful and more dangerous than they had realized. The crowds saw him and remembered the old poem that had prophesied a king so humble that he rode not a chariot, but a donkey.

They were right to recognize him as their king, but they missed the point about the donkey. The crowds thought it was time for God to overthrow the Roman legions, and they cheered Jesus as if he were a guerrilla leader in from the hills to take the city. When they realized their mistake, they turned away and forgot him.

But the authorities did not forget him. They realized at last the threat that Jesus represented, and began to lay their plans to remove him from the scene.

- - - - - - -

Were the Romans right to see Jesus as a threat to their power? Why?

- - - - - - -

Jesus had made his own plans. He was determined to celebrate one last Passover feast with his friends. He and his closest companions sought out a house where they could come and go without being seen, and ordered the preparations to be made. A dinner had to be prepared and matzoh, the unleavened bread which served as a reminder of the flight from Egypt, had to be bought. The upstairs room where they were to gather needed to be decorated for the holiday. Jesus sent Peter and John to make the necessary arrangements.

Jesus knew that he could not avoid the inevitable confrontation with the Roman authorities for long, but he wanted so much to celebrate this meal. By now, it was clear to him that his days were numbered. He still believed in God's kingdom. He still held on to the hope that one day there would be an end to hunger and thirst, to war and suffering. But before that day came, he would die.

Jesus and his friends began their meal. They came to the part of the Passover service when all share the matzoh as a way to remember their ancestors' escape from slavery. Jesus was presiding at the table. He took the piece of unleavened bread and said the ancient blessing: "You are blessed, Lord our God, King of the universe, who bring forth bread from the earth."

The bread was about to be broken. So was Jesus also to be broken. He realized that his friends would never again celebrate Passover without remembering this meal with him, and he understood that those who trusted him could see the beginning of the kingdom of God. God's will was already being done. Whenever hungry people were fed, lonely people were comforted, the sick were made well, and peace prevailed, God's will was being fulfilled. God's kingdom was being born. For Jesus' followers it was as important to remember what he had done as it was to remember that escape from Egypt. Something new was taking place during this holiday. Jesus was becoming the center and the focus of God's dreams for the world.

The Bread of Life

Jesus looked at the bread in his hand and slowly, firmly, broke it. He glanced around the table at the friends who were with him. "Take this and eat it," he said. "This is my body, which is being given for you. Do this in remembering me."

Those were Jesus' own words, not the words of the Passover ritual. His friends must have looked at each other with surprise, wondering what he could mean.

Later Jesus lifted the cup of wine to say the old blessing. "You are blessed, Lord our God, King of the universe, who give us the fruit of the vine." He looked into the cup at the dark red wine. Blood. It was a preview of his own death he saw in that cup. "This is my blood," he said. "It is about to be poured out for you and for many. Drink this cup to remember me."

The meal drew to its close. It would have been pleasant to stay in this setting for the rest of the night – surrounded by friends, comfortable and drowsy at the end of a long meal. But that would be too dangerous. In spite of the precautions his followers had taken, someone might have seen them. So with the determination of people who must be on their way, they said their farewells. As they were preparing to leave, the man named Judas seemed angry with Jesus, and Jesus had spoken harshly to him. Their conversation made very little sense to the others, but Judas went off alone. Jesus and his closest friends crept through the ominous, pitch-dark streets to the city gate, made their way through – did anyone recognize them? – and at last came to an olive orchard called Gethsemane, just a short distance from the city. When the sun came up in the morning, they would have a magnificent view of the temple, across the valley from where they were camping. For now, the orchard seemed deserted. It appeared as a refuge, a sanctuary from the fear they all felt. Surely here they were safe. Here they could relax, and be at peace.

§

Only a few days later, the nightmare of that last supper with Jesus had been changed forever by the news that God had raised him from the dead. It took a while for them all to believe it, and no wonder! What would you have said if word began to spread that your leader, executed as a criminal, had been seen alive?

Many of Jesus' companions left Jerusalem after he died. They must have felt out of place in the city. They were country people, more at home among the boats and fisherfolk of the little villages by the Sea of Galilee, or working the land, tending their flocks and herds.

Two such people were on their way home on the Sunday after Jesus' death. One was named Cleopas.

The Bread of Life

The name of the other has been forgotten. All we know about them is that they had been followers of Jesus. They had trusted his dream and been crushed by the news of his arrest and death. They had heard the rumors that he had been seen, but of course they could not take them seriously. So they set out on the long, lonely journey home.

As they were traveling along the dusty road through the hills beyond Jerusalem, a stranger joined them. It was not unusual for travelers who were alone to attach themselves to groups of people on the road; it was safer, and provided company besides. So the three of them went on together. Cleopas and his friend were eager to share the story of what had happened to Jesus, and wondered how this stranger could have missed hearing about him.

It began to grow dark. They had come to the inn of a village called Emmaus. The stranger stood there waiting, giving Cleopas and his companion the choice of whether to invite him to join them. They urged the stranger not to risk traveling alone in the dark, so he agreed to stay with them. They prepared to share their evening meal together. As they began, the stranger took bread, spoke the words of blessing – "You are blessed, Lord our God, King of the universe, who bring forth bread from the earth." At that moment they knew him. But then Jesus was gone. He had made himself known to them in the breaking of bread. They needed no other sign.

§

Years passed, and the movement that began with Jesus' friends spread from town to town. Soon Christians could be found in every city of the Roman Empire. People carried their faith with them to the very edges of the Roman world. Instead of a few dozen disciples, the followers of Jesus numbered in the thousands, and then the millions.

Many things changed about being a Christian. The first followers of Jesus met in secret and in fear for their lives. Yet within a few hundred years emperors were building vast cathedrals and bishops became honored members of their courts. However, some things did not change. When the first followers of Jesus met together, they continued to share bread and wine. They offered their thanksgiving for God's gifts, and they remembered especially the life, death and resurrection of Jesus. They believed that when they followed Jesus' command to "do this" he was there with them.

Jesus' followers faced terror and torture. They were often arrested and jailed, even executed. Some of them were crucified in a mockery of Jesus' own death. The remarkable thing about the beginning of Christianity is that all the persecutions could not kill the church. To the contrary, it grew stronger. If you had asked those first faithful people why they were so strong, I believe they would have answered that Christ was at their side. They were certain that Christ fed them with his own strength. They touched him, and found the courage that was his to offer, whenever they ate the bread and drank the wine he had offered them at his last supper.

Christians keep on eating the bread and drinking the wine. In isolated mountain villages, on caravans winding their way through the desert, in the slums of filthy cities, and in royal palaces, the words echo down through time: "This is my body. This is my blood." The hands that break the bread are brown, and black, and white, and yellow, and red. They are scarred and calloused, smooth and jeweled, young and strong, twisted with old age. Jesus offered his friends a way to remember him and to find him present with them. They accepted his invitation. They still do.

§

Christians find that sharing bread and wine is the best way they have to meet Jesus. It is one of the ways he chose to be with us. It might seem to be a strange way to worship: eating bread and drinking wine are, after all, so ordinary.

But that is just the point. Jesus did not describe some strange, painful or dangerous rite for his followers. He took the things that are most natural to human beings – eating and drinking – and made them holy by pointing out that when we do them with other Christians, he himself is there. Christ's presence feeds us and gives us drink. That is not just a pious comment; it is the truth which countless Christians have found to be true. When we share this simple meal, the very life of Christ – his body and blood, his own identity – are as close to us as the bread we eat and the wine we drink.

Most of the people who read this book have probably never experienced hunger more severe than skipping a meal. We belong to a place and time where hunger is something that happens to other people. But that has not always been true for Christians. Our ancestors in faith knew what it was like to be hungry. Even today, there are millions of Christians in Latin America, Africa, Asia, and even in our own country who have never – *never in their lives* – known what it is to have enough to eat.

That fact makes the means Jesus chose to be present with us all the more important and meaningful. God's will is for all people to live in freedom, in a land flowing with milk and honey. The bread and wine we share is a sign of God's intention for the human family. It is a reminder of the promise of the kingdom of God. In our meal of bread and wine we meet a God who feeds us. That is a God whose love is real.

- - - - - - -

Gandhi, the great liberator of the Indian people, once remarked that in a world where so many people are starving, the only form in which God would dare appear is bread. What do you think he meant by those words? Do you agree?

As Our Savior Christ Has Taught Us, We Now Pray . . .

Fred could hardly believe he had forgotten anything as important as a geometry exam. He sat stunned at his desk as Mrs. Washington came down the aisle, passing out tests. He wasn't even sure how much the test would cover. It wasn't as if geometry were like English or history; he looked forward to them, and he always got the point. Geometry was hard work. It never made sense on the first try. Fred's earlier test grades had taught him that he needed to work hard to make it through.

As the teacher drew nearer, Fred's stomach tightened, and when he took his copy of the exam, he noticed that his hands were sweating. There was only one thing to do. He closed his eyes tightly. "God," he prayed, "I'm sorry I forgot this test, but I really do need a good grade. So please, let me pass. Let me do more than pass. Please give me at least a B. Amen."

One of Fred's troubles with geometry was that he was never sure whether he was right or not. After school, he and two of his friends tried to remember how they had completed the problems, but Fred couldn't even remember his answers. He was worried, but still, at least he had prayed. If he was lucky, God would help him out and Mrs. Washington would never know he had forgotten to study.

The exams were returned at the end of the following week. Once again, Fred noticed his hands were sweating as the tests were passed out. At the top of his paper Mrs. Washington had written, "Please see me after class."

"Fred," his teacher said when the bell had rung and they were alone, "I know geometry isn't your favorite subject. I know it's not your easiest subject, either. But what happened? You didn't solve a single problem completely."

"Mrs. Washington, I forgot about the test," Fred said, staring at the top of her desk.

"Well, Fred, I'm sorry, but it's not as if I hadn't given you plenty of warning. I was afraid you'd tell me something like that. All I can say is, I hope your next exam is a lot better, or you're going to end up with a real disappointment at the end of the year."

Fred left the classroom with a heavy heart. His grade for the term was ruined, and his parents would be angry. His friends would think he was really stupid to have forgotten a test like that one. And where was God when he needed him? Fred remembered vividly the sermon about prayer Fr. Ritter had preached a few Sundays before. Fred had been an acolyte that morning, so he had been right next to the pulpit. He could distinctly remember Fr. Ritter saying, "Most of the time prayer fails because we don't pray hard enough. We don't really believe God's promises." Well, Fred had given God a great big chance. He had really depended on him. And God had let him down.

On Sunday morning his father knocked on his door. "Fred," he said, "if you don't get up, you'll never be ready to leave with us for church."

"I'm not going," Fred replied from inside his room.

"What do you mean, you're not going? You're scheduled to read the lesson," his father reminded him.

"I don't care," Fred said. "I don't think I'm going to go to church for a while. What good does it do you?"

- - - - - - -

Was Fred right to blame God for not giving him a passing grade?

Was Fr. Ritter right to claim that prayers don't succeed because people don't pray hard or confidently enough?

- - - - - - -

Both Fred and Fr. Ritter – and probably a great many Christians – assume that the purpose of prayer is to ask favors from God. The favor may be something we want either for ourselves or someone else: a car, a bicycle, a place on the debating team. Or it may be a request for God to fix things: a broken arm, an argument with your mother. There is a place for prayers like that; sometimes they are an honest effort to share our feelings with God. Even Jesus sometimes prayed that way. The New Testament tells us that the night before he died, he prayed so hard that his sweat was like blood. It also tells us that he prayed: "Father, take this cup away from me."

But even though we mean well when we pray those

prayers, we must be very careful just exactly what we are asking for. Are we really wishing for God to short-circuit nature?

One of the unpleasant truths about being human is that our bodies are subject to all kinds of ailments. Some of them we bring on ourselves. Many of them are partly our fault. Still others come to us by accident. But whatever the cause, our bodies hurt, and at last they fail altogether. When we ask God for healing, are we really asking that he re-make us in some other form? God does not tamper with nature.

After all, we live in a world where actions have consequences. If I strike you in the face, you will be hurt and probably bruised. It does me no good to ask God to make you well. I must bear the consequences of my act. If you make an unkind remark about me that hurts me deeply, it is useless to ask God to take away the pain.

There is a very serious reason why this is so. If God intervened – we might say *meddled* – every time someone did something with painful consequences, we would no longer be free. Part of the freedom with which God has blessed us is the freedom to cause pain to ourselves and to others. We are free only if our actions have real consequences. If God is going to come along and tidy up after us, we are not free at all. We are children running loose in a nursery with an over-patient parent to spoil us and clean up after us.

§

There is more to prayer than asking God for favors. We think of prayer as a special form of communication, or even conversation, between ourselves and God. That is true as far as it goes. But prayer is really whatever we do that makes us more aware of God and our relationship with him. We are conscious of that relationship in many ways. Often we put it into words, silently or out loud. But prayer doesn't need words to be real. Whenever we are aware of God, we are at prayer.

That is true because God is not just the creative and loving power "out there" which brings the universe into being. If that were true, we would really have very little to do with God. He would be like an absentee landlord, making his presence felt from time to time, but rarely on hand when we needed him.

That is not the God we Christians have learned to trust. God has been "on hand" since the beginning. In Jesus, God drew so near that he lived among us and even died a fully human death.

But even that isn't all. God's creative love is the *environment* in which we live. Our ancestors used the word "spirit" to talk about God, because they came to understand that you can't pin God down to any one place. When they looked for something to explain what they meant, they thought of "breath," or "wind." We can't really see our breath, but we can certainly feel its effects. It can serve as a sign of the life within us. As we say, "As long as there's breath in me," I am still alive.

Wind, like breath, is invisible, but we can also feel its effects. It is powerful, yet also strangely refreshing. (Have you ever felt the brisk surge of energy a blast of cold air can bring to life?) Wind is really only the air we breathe; yet when that air begins to move, there is action, power and enormous energy. *Wind* and *breath* are really the same thing, felt outside our bodies and also within them.

No wonder our ancestors compared God to the lively, evermoving air. God the Spirit fills us with life, enters deep inside us to keep us alive; but God is also around us, the loving energy which breathes life into the whole creation. That's true whether we notice it or not.

Prayer is what we call the special awareness we have of this God who is always within us. Christians have noticed that we pray different kinds of prayer depending upon how we experience God and are relating ourselves to him.

The primary form of prayer is *worship*. This prayer has its origin in our awareness of what God is like. There are times when we are amazed at the extent of God's love, or at the ways in which God gives meaning to our life, or at the astonishing variety of creativity life offers us. When we are aware of what God is really like, it is the most natural thing in the world to worship. Sometimes our feelings take over and even do our praying for us. You might be moved by the wonder of nature – a sunset, or a newborn animal; you might be overwhelmed at the sight of the ocean, limitless and awesome. You might put your feelings of reverence or praise into words, but even if you don't you are still praying.

Thanksgiving is not very different from worship, but it is a kind of prayer that is in response to something more specific that brings us closer to God. It could be recovery from an illness, so that we discover all over again how precious is God's gift of life. Or we might have good news that will change our future. We may have discovered that someone loves us. Our natural response in such moments is to thank God.

Whenever Christians offer thanksgiving, sooner or later they remember the special gift which the life and death of Jesus signify for us. When we eat bread and drink wine together, we give thanks for these gifts. In fact, we call that meal the *Eucharist*, the word for *thanksgiving* in Greek – the language in which the early Christians prayed and worshipped.

Still another form of prayer is *confession*. This is the form our relationship with God takes when we are conscious of how far we fall short of the intentions God has for us. Each one of us has some sense of the potential that God has given us simply because we bear God's image: the opportunities to be creative; to live a meaningful life; to be people of love. All of us are well aware of the ways in which we fail God and God's image in us, and of the pain our failures cause ourselves and others.

When we do, we are sometimes overwhelmed by guilt. We recognize that if God were vindictive, we would deserve to be punished. But alongside our guilt, we recall God's mercy. We know that our God is a loving and forgiving God, and this knowledge is also a dimension of our prayer. The deeper our confession, the more certain we become that we are forgiven, and the more grateful we are that God lifts the weight of our guilt.

There is another kind of prayer which legitimately *asks God for favors*. It is in some ways the most difficult form of prayer. It is so easy to fall into selfish prayer, which is trying to use God to make things happen for our convenience. ("Please, God, don't let it rain on my picnic.") Rain is the result of natural forces obeying their own rhythms, and is absolutely necessary if the earth is to feed its people. Do we really expect God to reorganize the whole of nature to fit our schedule? Isn't that wishful thinking? Or, worse, aren't we trying to *use* God to manipulate the universe according to our own private wants and needs?

So when we dare to pray this kind of prayer, it is especially important to be honest – with ourselves, and with God. There is nothing wrong with sharing our hopes and wishes with God, even when they ask for what we assume is impossible, or for something God could not do without violating his own nature and the patterns of the universe. Even Jesus once asked God to take away his suffering, as he prayed in the garden of Gethsemane. But then he added something more: "Nevertheless, not what I want, but what you will." Jesus shrank from his pain just as we would; he wished it could be possible to escape it, and he shared that wish with God. But he also knew that if he had fled from pain, his life's work would have been unfinished. He would have failed to show the full nature of love, God's and his own. So although he prayed a very human wish – "Take this cup from me" – he also asked that God's will be done for his life.

That kind of praying isn't always easy. Having to face the fact that we aren't going to get what we want can make us feel alone, disappointed, even angry with

God. As he was dying on the cross, Jesus himself prayed, "My God, my God, why have you forsaken me?" Of course, God had not really forsaken him; God was never nearer than when Jesus was dying on his cross. Yet Jesus felt as if he were all alone, so he shared the bitterness and the terror of that moment with God.

But we don't just pray out of selfishness, or disappointment. We also pray because we care about people, and want the best for them. That kind of prayer brings us closer to one another, because it places our caring within the setting of God's love for us. It is a way of sharing our love and concern with God. It deepens our love, and strengthens the community between us. It affects not only the person we pray for, but also changes us.

Yet even those prayers don't always produce the results we hope for. Then we are really disappointed, and perhaps confused as well. Why, we ask, should God not hear our prayer when we ask him to heal someone who is suffering? Surely pain is not God's will for the human family?

Jesus has shown us clearly that suffering can never be God's will. The dream of the kingdom of God holds up for us a way of living where all pain and sickness are forgotten. Where God's will is done, there is no suffering. Whenever illness or disease

[105]

strikes, God's will is being violated. It is *always* appropriate to pray for healing, but only if we are clear about what we mean by healing.

If we recall the story of the paralyzed man whom Jesus healed, we can learn a great deal about the nature of illness and healing. Before Jesus paid any attention to the symptoms which had crippled the man, he assured him that his sins were forgiven. In Jesus' mind, the most important fact about the man's healing was not whether or not he could walk again. It was the man's spiritual well-being; whether or not he was at peace with himself, with God and with the human family. That peace is what matters most.

The truth is, we still don't understand much about healing. Even the best doctors are painfully aware of how little they can do to cure illness or disease. There seems to be a powerful impulse in the human spirit towards health and wholeness, related to the creativity we identify as God's image within us. That creative desire for well-being is strengthened in many ways: through the use of medicines; by the positive attitude of the person who is ill; and especially by the care and love of people who surround the person with concern and human warmth. Praying for one another in times of illness is one of the most loving, and therefore healing, acts we can perform. Often it becomes one of the means by which God's will is done and the disease or illness disappears.

Yet sometimes the symptoms do not go away. They grow worse, and eventually the person dies. It is easy for us to see that death as a failure of prayer – but we would be wrong. Our bodies die; that is their end, because they are part of a world in which the process of nature inevitably leads to death. It is as selfish and unrealistic to ask God to set that process aside as it is to ask him to rearrange the rain for our picnic. Healing is more than the relieving of symptoms. Healing restores the bond of peace with ourselves and with God that makes it possible to die knowing we are loved.

Every time Christians gather to worship, they pray for those who are sick. Some will recover; soon they will be back at their old place in church, almost as if nothing had ever been wrong. Others will weaken, and die, their bodies will return to the earth, and they will be missed and mourned. But if our prayers are honest, all will have been helped towards healing, because all will have been surrounded by a community of care which makes God's love real for them. And that makes all the difference.

§

We should not be surprised if we wonder about prayer. Jesus' own friends asked him how to pray. In response, he gave them what has always been the model of prayer. You have probably known it as long as you can remember.

"When you pray," Jesus told them, "say 'Our father.' "

§

When we begin our prayers as Jesus taught, it may seem as if we are only trying to get God's attention, like placing a telephone call. But Jesus meant something else. Prayer is the way by which we come to see more clearly the way things are. God is the beginning and the ending of all things. Although we forget it, the whole creation owes its existence to God. That is why true prayer begins with a reminder of who God is.

But not only do we begin by remembering God; we begin by remembering that we are bound to God. The God to whom we pray is not an impersonal force, but a Presence to whom we are as closely bound as to any human being – even those to whom we owe our life and identity. Prayer is the way by which we remember God, and the bonds which hold us together. Prayer is the way by which we recall the truth about God, and about ourselves.

Sometimes we speak our prayers. We also sing them, dance them, shout them, let them brood silently. But whatever form they take, they change things. Most of all, they change *us*. The more we pray, and the more honestly we pray, the more clearly we see, the more fully we understand, and the more deeply we love.

PART THREE

Will you persevere in resisting evil, and, whenever you
fall into sin, repent and return to the Lord?

I will, with God's help.

This Fragile Earth,
Our Island Home

If you were to dive to the sea floor, you would find yourself in an environment radically different from the one you live in. Without carefully-tended equipment, you would die. But if you made use of your own skill and the techniques developed by under-water experts, you would discover a part of the universe inhabited by creatures unlike any you had ever seen before. The ocean's depths have proven to be the breeding ground for marine life, both plants and animals, which are more ingenious and unexpected than anything an artist could have devised.

The first explorers from Europe who came upon the New World must have had much the same feelings when they discovered the living things that grow in the Americas. Both animals and plant life were different from anything they knew. Europeans even thought that tomatoes were poison!

When those first visitors met the people and moved among the forms of life they had never seen before, they found them strange and alien. The Europeans treated them as if they had nothing in common with them. They considered the native Americans sub-human creatures; the explorers even argued about whether they had souls! The original inhabitants of the Americas were enslaved, their possessions seized, and for many years they were displayed in Europe like specimens in a zoo.

We might well ask how those first adventurers could have been so cruel to a people who welcomed them with wonder and hospitality. Surely the answer lies in the fact that the Europeans saw their victims as different, and therefore as unrelated to them. Because they set themselves apart from these "others," Europeans believed they could do with them whatever they pleased. It was the same attitude that led the settlers on the frontier to believe they could plow up the whole mid-section of the United States, destroying the natural vegetation in the process, and to slaughter whatever animals they came upon because they were there for the taking.

Whenever human beings distance themselves from the rest of the creation, it becomes easy to believe they can do whatever they want with the world and its creatures. When we behave towards other people as if we had nothing in common with them, we are overlooking the fact that we share *life*. The same is true of other living things, our "co-creatures." As bizarre and curious as those microscopic organisms and blind fish that lurk on the ocean floor may appear, we and they are bound together because we are living beings. If we were to discover life on another planet, or buried deep within another galaxy, we would still be bound to that life because we share it. We who are human are in no way separated or distanced from the rest of the universe. The same life that teems in a drop of water, or in the thin air of a mountain, thrives in our spirits.

The more we think about the ties that bind us to all living creatures, the more we realize that the world is truly what science calls an *ecosystem*. In an ecosystem each part of the whole of nature depends upon the rest, and if one tiny segment of the web of life is changed or damaged, there will be effects throughout the system.

We have found evidence for this fact in a great many different places. Chemicals released into the atmosphere in one location come down with the rain many hundreds of miles away. They are swept into the great rivers and carried still further from their source. Eventually they seep into the earth, and reappear in the vegetation. Animals which rely on plant life for their food then ingest the chemicals, and in turn pass them along the food chain. Long after their original source has been forgotten, these poisons remain to inflict illness and even death on the human population.

The worst, the most terrifying, evidence of the way all living things are dependent on one another comes from scientists who warn us of the effects of a nuclear war. Devastating as it would be, the worst damage from the explosion of a nuclear bomb would not be the millions of deaths and injuries inflicted at the site of the detonation. Rather, the long-term terror would come from the damage to human, animal and plant life in the aftermath. Many experts believe that even a limited thermonuclear war would destroy all life on the planet by spreading deadly radioactive poison throughout the earth and altering the ozone layer, which protects us from the sun's rays. It is ironic that our century, which has produced so much new information and so many amazing advances in technology, now understands for the first time the true bonds that hold us together. It is the threat of universal destruction that makes the point most clearly.

This deepened sense that all of life is held together contrasts sharply with what many people have always believed. For a long time, our civilization taught us that human beings are "above" the rest of creation, that we are invincible, and that our power gives us the right to do whatever we want with nature. Human beings have slaughtered some animal species to the point of extinction, for food or even for sport. They continue to dig up the riches from earth's heart, leaving behind disfiguring scars which appear as great gouges on the face of our planet. In ripping up earth's surface, they destroy forests and create the conditions which lead to draught and even famine.

But Christian faith holds to a very different vision of the natural world and our relationship to it. Our ancestors kept that vision alive by telling and retelling this story about the creation of the world.

§

These are the generations of the heavens and of the earth when they were created. In the day that the Lord God made the earth and the heavens, when no plants of the field were in the earth and no grass had sprung up (since the Lord God had not caused it to rain on the earth, and there was no one to till the ground; but a mist rose from the earth and watered its face) – then the Lord God formed the human from the ground, and breathed the breath of life into the human's nostrils; and the human became a living being. And the Lord God planted a garden in Eden, in the east; and there he put the human being whom he had created. And out of the ground the Lord God made to grow every plant which is attractive and good for food, and also in the midst of the garden the tree of life and the tree of the knowledge of good and evil.

The Lord God put the human being into the garden of Eden to till it and keep it. Then the Lord God said, "It is not good for the human to be alone; I will make an appropriate companion." So out of the ground the Lord God formed every beast of the countryside and every bird of the air, and brought them to the human to see what their name would be; and whatever the human being called the creature, that was its name.

§

We can catch some of the playful spirit the story-tellers who invented this tale must have put into it. It is fun to imagine the first human being giving names to all the creatures of the animal kingdom – "I think I'll call this one a crocodile" – and relishing the lush abundance of a garden from which nothing is left out.

But there is more to the story from the Book of

Genesis than an imagination enjoying its own creativity. The teller of this tale also intended to describe
how things are supposed to be. In the garden, all that
lives is in harmony with the rest of creation. There is
no death, no violence, and no greed. The human
being lives among the other living beings without fear.
On the other hand, the rest of the natural world need
fear nothing from the human. To the contrary, the
role of the human being in the garden is that of a
gardener – a responsible overseer. God entrusts the
human being with power over the garden. It is the
human who gives the other creatures their names.
But that power is meant to be power for good; the
human being must care for the garden, till it and
monitor its growth. The purpose of human life
described in this very old story is found in the image
of humankind as *steward* – the caretaker who watches
over the owner's property in his absence. But there is
no question of who the owner is. It is God's garden.
The human being, like the rest of the inhabitants of
the garden, owes his existence to the breath which the
Lord God has breathed into him. Every being in the
garden is alive because of the gift of God's life-giving
spirit.

It is as if God had entrusted the human being with
the assignment of working alongside God in creating a
good and abundant earth. The human being is en-
titled to enjoy the garden, to feast on its produce and
to appreciate its beauty. But with that privilege comes

the responsibility to preserve and develop its fruitfulness and harmony.

§

This ancient story of creation tries to put into words a vision of how human beings are meant to live on earth. Although the implications are spelled out in story form, they are quite clear.

After a number of false starts, which explains why there are so many different kinds of creatures on the earth, the Lord God had not yet succeeded in finding an appropriate companion for the human being. Finally, God put his creature into a deep sleep, removed a rib from his side, and formed another human being from it. When he awakened, the human was delighted. At last there was someone to share his life. The man and the woman belonged together.

§

What makes the man and the woman different from all the other creatures in the garden is that they are aware of their responsibility. The root of their responsibility is their *freedom*. Because they are free, they have a special power over everything in the garden. They can either care for the rest of nature, as God intends, or they can abuse the earth and its creatures for their own benefit. But the abuse of that freedom brings terrible consequences. Should the man and the woman abuse their power, the order and harmony of nature would be destroyed. Pain would replace harmony, ugliness triumph over beauty. Most of all, the human beings would suffer too. They might believe that mistreating nature and doing as they pleased could never hurt them, but they would live to regret those actions. Nature would no longer be a perfectly hospitable environment. It would shut them out of its embrace, and the man and the woman would find themselves wandering over the earth in need and suffering.

It is remarkable how clearly those long-dead storytellers saw the consequences of the abuse of human freedom. Like the man and the woman who allowed their greed and power to get the best of them, the human family has chosen to plunder rather than to nurture the earth. Like those two figures in the story who suffered for their wrong, and were condemned to look back at Eden with longing, we can only regret what has already been done to the earth. But like them, we still bear the responsibility for the earth. Its future remains in our hands. We human beings are still called by God to be earth's gardeners and its caretakers. Even now, it is not too late.

Christians in the twentieth century have learned to take those stories at the beginning of the Book of Genesis very seriously. Once it becomes clear that the future of the earth rests with us, the theme of the stories makes a great deal of sense. The more we understand that the planet earth is our "island home," on which we are all bound to live together, the more fragile life seems to be. We are coming to appreciate how challenging a gift freedom is.

Yet as we think through the implications of these stories for us, we can take heart by remembering that God gives freedom to the human race because God has hopes for us. Our freedom is not meant to be an unbearable burden, or a possession so frightening we have to give it back. We are free because God approves of what we can do for the earth in his name. Now that we have come to perceive that its future rests with us, we can begin to develop the talents that will be required of us as good stewards.

- - - - - - -

What do you consider to be the greatest threats to the survival of the planet and its life?

How do you share in the pollution and destruction of the earth?

What might we human beings do to care properly for the earth?

What special gifts do you have for caring for the earth?

[122]

The Facts of Life:
Evil, Sin and Death

Jennifer had never known anyone with cancer until her grandmother went to the hospital. Everyone had been noticing that Grandma didn't seem to eat as much as she once did, and after dinner she often had to go and lie down. Grandma always hated to go to the doctor, but one day when Jennifer got home, she found her mother helping to pack a suitcase. "Grandma's been to the doctor and he says she needs some tests done at the hospital," her mother said briskly. Jennifer thought that her mother sounded the way she always did when she was worried but didn't want anyone to know it.

Her grandmother only stayed in the hospital a week, but before her homecoming Jennifer's parents called all the children into the living room. "Grandma's tests are finished," her mother began, and tears began welling up in her eyes. A cold fear clutched Jennifer's stomach.

"The doctor says Grandma has cancer," her father said quietly. "He was in today and explained to Grandma just what is the matter with her, and he says there's no reason why she can't come home now. Later she may have to go back to the hospital, but for the time being there is nothing they can do for her there that can't be done right here at home."

Jennifer wasted no time getting home from school the next day. There was Grandma, sitting on the sofa with her feet up, looking no different than she had when she went to the hospital a week before. Jennifer gave her a hug, and began to cry. "Oh, Jennifer," her grandmother said, "I want this to be a special time for us."

And it was. Over the next weeks, Grandma gradually got weaker and thinner. One day she announced that she could not make it downstairs, and from then on she stayed in her room. Life became very different for Jennifer and her family. Sometimes things were hard. It was not always easy to remember not to make too much noise. Jennifer's friends seemed to hesitate to come to her house. There were meals to be carried upstairs, dishes to be taken down. But there were also wonderful times when Grandma just sat and talked. Jennifer liked it best when it was just the two of them. Sometimes she told her grandmother what she would like to imagine for herself when she was grown, and her grandmother would reminisce about when she had been a girl and had first left home.

When her grandmother died two months later, Jennifer was filled with grief that she was gone. She realized that she had grown closer to her grandmother than she had ever been before. In the weeks that followed, Jennifer dreamed often about her grandmother. Sometimes she would wake up, her eyes moist; it was as if Grandma had been *right there*. "And where is she really?" Jennifer asked herself. "What's happened to her? Can she still hear me? Can she *see* me? Did she meet Grandad, like everyone says? What is it like to die?"

§

The death of her grandmother brought Jennifer face to face with one of the most basic facts of life: people die. She had known that for years, of course. She had laughed as a small child when cartoon figures went to their death. Later, she had watched countless hours of television shows in which people were shot, knifed, or otherwise killed. Newscasts even depicted the deaths of real people, in flaming crashes or on some battlefield thousands of miles away. Now, for the first time, Jennifer was meeting death in her own family circle. Her grandmother was gone; on this earth she would never see her again. Her grandmother would not be there when Jennifer graduated from high school. She would never see her dressed for her senior prom, never hear from Jennifer when she got her first job. When she remembered all the places from which her grandmother would now be absent forever, Jennifer was angry and sad. She tried hard to make sense of it, but it seemed so unfair. Why should people have to die?

§

Jennifer's questions and anger about the fact of death are not new. When our ancestors imagined the perfect garden which was the human family's first home, they depicted it as a place without death. There was a tree in the garden, the tree of life; as long as the man and the woman kept eating from its fruit, they would live forever. The garden was not only a place of harmony; it was also a setting untouched by pain or sorrow. There was no grief in the garden, because everything lasted for all eternity.

That vision of unity is a far cry from the universe as we know it. Not only is the human family constantly torn by violence and bloodshed; the whole of nature, to the farthest reaches of the cosmos, is at war. One poet who thought deeply about the cruelty of the natural world described creation as "red in tooth and claw." He was reflecting upon the chain that stretches from the simplest form of life to the most complex, in which each level feeds by devouring those beneath.

The same violence spreads to the edges of space. Planets collide with one another and are destroyed. Many of the heavenly bodies we see on a starry night, which seem so moving and magnificent, are in fact the product of mighty explosions and bursts of destructive energy.

This is the way the world is. This is the way the universe is put together. It is a fact of life that death and violence pervade the whole creation.

We experience death as a symptom of this chaotic disorder, which extends everywhere. There is nothing necessarily destructive about death in itself; plants pass through the cycle of their natural growth and at last they die. But their seeds and bulbs have long since been dispersed, and new trees and plants grow to take their place. Even animals that have completed their natural life span grow old and die peacefully, as if they were prepared for it by instinct.

But human beings are different. For us, death is not a matter of instinct. We experience death as painful and unjust, because it always wounds us. When people die, relationships are broken. We are lonely, and our memories can never make up for the loss. Even if we find other friends, or form new relationships, no person can replace another. We are unique, and the ties that bind us to one another are an expression of that uniqueness.

- - - - - - -

Has anyone close to you died?

Has death affected your life? How?

- - - - - - -

Why is the universe a place of conflict and death? Our ancestors put the responsibility squarely on the man and the woman in the garden. Only one tree was forbidden them: the tree of the knowledge of good and evil. God warned them that if they ate from that tree, they would be punished. They would not believe it, and ate its fruit.

God was right. They now knew the difference between good and evil; they could experience pain as well as pleasure. But they also found death, because God banished them from the garden. They could no longer eat from the tree of life; they grew old and at last they died. God placed an angel with a flaming sword at the entrance of the garden, so that no one could ever again gain access to the tree of life. Death has become part of life, and pain has entered the human story.

§

Of course, we no longer believe that death is God's punishment for disobedience. We know that the very process of evolution, by which we believe God calls life into existence, has been a constant process of bringing forth life from conflict and death. Death is "natural" in that it has always been part of nature.

Yet the story also affirms that God's ultimate will for the universe is peace, not violence; harmony, not conflict. The garden of Eden is not so much where we came from as it is an expression of our belief that God really wants a universe without pain and loneliness.

You might even say that the violent universe in which we live is the raw material out of which God creates his perfect kingdom. The kingdom of God is the setting in which life can be lived without hate, pain or death.

The authors of the Book of Genesis seem to think that the knowledge of good and evil is more trouble than it is worth. But we might also consider that this knowledge is an image of freedom. Until we can tell the difference between good and evil, we are not really free. That freedom is part of the image of God we bear. It sets us apart from the rest of creation.

But the story-teller is right: that knowledge gets us into trouble. The problem with freedom is that we can choose either *good* – that is, we can decide to act in such a way that God's will is carried forward – or we can choose *evil* and behave in a way that is contrary to God's will. Human history tells us which choice human beings have usually made. In the early pages of Genesis, the two sons of the first human couple have an argument and Cain murders his brother Abel. The story-teller meant to show us that when confronted with the option of peace or violence, we often choose bloodshed.

The conflicts and choices that damage God's plans for the human family, as well as for the whole of creation, are what Christians mean by *sin*.

Some people try to define sin in terms of rules. They assume that God is like a somewhat eccentric high school principal with all the power to enforce his will. In fact, God is more like the author of a play. He gives the characters in his play the freedom either to behave in ways that bring love and justice into being, or to hurt one another. It is those destructive choices that are *sin*. They always have painful consequences, although they seem like good ideas at the time.

- - - - - -

Why do people choose evil over good?

Why do we choose wrongly even when we know better?

- - - - - -

Christians believe that God has always hoped for the best from humankind. We read our history as the story of life emerging out of death. We understand that the resurrection of Jesus is the best example of all the ways in which God continually works to bring into existence a human community in which pain and injustice are overcome.

We believe that we can share in that creative work, because God has given us the gift of freedom. If we are honest with ourselves, we must also admit that we tend to choose badly. We could help to build a more humane world if we chose. Peace and love are not just words to sing about. They are God's intentions for us.

Sin keeps getting in the way of those intentions. Rather than interrupt our freedom, God permits us to take actions (or neglect to do what we might) even if we do harm to God's own dreams. Rather than destroy our freedom, God permits us to wreck our own bodies. He watches as we inhale or ingest or inject poisons which cause illness and death. In the garden of Eden, tobacco and humans would have existed side by side; in the world we call home, we give ourselves lung cancer.

God even stands by while we do harm to others. He allows us to drink ourselves into oblivion, and then to drive a car down a crowded highway. Surely the carnage breaks God's heart, but so fiercely does he defend our freedom that even such sin does not tempt God to intrude.

Now the human family stands with the future of the planet earth in our hands. Surely God is holding his breath. He knows so well the past record we have when we make choices about good and evil.

And yet, God has still not given up hope. Knowing the power of sin, he has still not taken away our freedom.

We have not yet come to the end of our story – or of our rope. There is more to life than death and evil. We remain free. God still intends to see us through to the kingdom he meant for us from the beginning.

PART FOUR

Will you proclaim by word and example the Good News of God in Christ?

I will, with God's help.

Will you seek and serve Christ in all persons, loving your neighbor as yourself?

I will, with God's help.

Will you strive for justice and peace among all people, and respect the dignity of every human being?

I will, with God's help.

What Are We Living For?

Dear Mom and Dad,

By the time you read this, I will be gone. I hope you will forgive me for all the trouble I've caused you. I am sorry there is no way I can do this without making more trouble for you. Please understand that it's not your fault. It's just that my life doesn't have any meaning, and it seems a lot easier this way than to try to go on.

Your son,

Tom

What Are We Living For?

He read the letter through twice, folded it, and sealed it in an envelope. He walked downstairs to the kitchen and positioned it carefully on the table. Then he went back upstairs, to where he knew his mother kept her sleeping pills. He read the directions, and then, without hesitating, began to swallow them.

As he sat quietly waiting for sleep to come, Tom recalled again when he first wondered if his life was worth living. It had been last year, when he had unexpectedly panicked in the middle of his interview for a student exchange program. All through high school, he had been dreaming of spending his senior year abroad. Now anxiety broke over him like a wave. So much depended on this one interview! His breath came in short, painful gasps, his hands felt icy cold, and he realized his mind was empty. It was no surprise when a few weeks later a letter arrived, informing him that it was "not possible" to offer him a place in the exchange program. His dream was gone.

But that was only the beginning. Blinded by tears, he made his way to Susan's house to share with her the disappointment he felt. He rang the bell, and Sue appeared at the door. "Well, what's the matter with you?" she laughed. 'Did you just lose your last friend?"

"I'm not going away next year."

"Well, what's the big loss? Nobody wants to go away for senior year anyway."

"Sue, I've been counting on this trip for three years. Can I please come in and talk about it?"

"Well . . . . "

That was when he noticed the car in Sue's driveway. It belonged to Phil Stone; there was no mistaking it.

"Maybe I did lose my last friend," he mumbled, turning and heading down the steps.

It was true. Tom had been so elated when Sue began to go out with him that he hadn't really kept up with the friends he used to know. Now he realized there was no one else he wanted to see. His solitude clung to him as he made his way back home, climbed the stairs to his room, and closed the door behind him.

§

That had been the beginning. As the days and weeks went by, Tom realized that the people around him didn't seem to matter. Summer came and he went to work, as he had for several years, at the convenience store down the street. But he lost his job in July. The manager said the customers were complaining that Tom ignored them. Tom shrugged his shoulders, asked when he could come in to pick up his last check, and went home. He spent the rest of the summer in his room.

When his senior year began, Tom went through the motions of applying to college, but when he went for his interviews, he felt as if he had nothing to say. Of course his applications were turned down. When the time came for graduation pictures to be taken, only four students failed to show up. Tom was one of them.

Last night his mother had tried to talk to him about what he would do after graduation, but Tom had nothing to say. He didn't really want to do anything at all. His mother finally lost her temper and slammed the door as she left the room. That was when he made his decision.

§

He was in bed, and there were bars on both sides. He was reminded of the crib he had slept in as a small boy. The room was dark, but he could see his parents' faces. His father was crying.

"Oh, son," his mother said. "There are so many things to live for."

"Like what?" he asked.

§

Tom had discovered for himself what we all have to face: a sense of purpose can really be a matter of life and death. How else can our lives have meaning? Knowing what we are living for makes all the difference between being really alive and merely existing. The most extreme response to a meaningless life is suicide. Most people never reach that point, but we are probably all familiar with Tom's question: *What am I living for?*

Just because it is such an important question, many people never have the courage to ask themselves if the purpose they live for is worth their efforts. We set out to win friends, or to achieve popularity. We seek to accumulate power, or persuade ourselves that the secret of a more meaningful life will be found in more and more possessions. Even though we should be able to remember what a let-down Christmas afternoon usually is, we tell ourselves that if only we have a new car, or stereo, or a bigger and better bike, we will be able to live with enthusiasm and excitement.

Sometimes people do face the failure of their goals, and fall into despair. In order to mask the pain of not knowing why they are living, they try to find ways to deaden their senses. Alcohol, drugs or an endless search for thrills and excitement can sometimes appear to offer a way to forget how purposeless life seems. The problem is, none of them really works. They merely become part of the problem.

- - - - - - -

How would you describe your own goals in life? What gives your life its meaning?

Why do you think that teenagers abuse drugs or alcohol?

- - - - - - -

There is something about being human that makes us tend to miss the purpose that would really make life worth living. We understand how many opportunities we have for making the human family a more humane and loving community in which to live. We know perfectly well that God has given us the freedom to work towards building a world fit for human beings to live in. Yet we keep choosing wrongly. This tendency to make the wrong decisions is what Christians call *original sin*. It isn't something we've learned or grown to love. It has been with us from the beginning.

Jesus was very well aware of this habit we have of choosing to behave in ways that destroy our future.

Although he knew it, he was never shocked by it, and he always invited people to start over. Jesus took his friends as they were, knowing the worst about them, and gave them the chance to change – even when they failed.

Simon Peter, the fisherman who was one of Jesus' oldest and best friends, is a good example. Simon always meant well, and yet he almost never got the point. When Jesus gradually came to understand that his fate would take him to Jersualem and an inevitable confrontation with death, Simon Peter tried to talk him out of the journey. At the last supper with his friends, Jesus performed a traditional act of hospitality, which was ordinarily done by servants: he washed his friends' feet. Jesus was trying to show them how much he cared about them, but when it came to be Peter's turn he said, "You will never wash my feet." Jesus replied that if Peter would not let him perform that act of service for him, they really weren't friends at all.

The most dramatic failure of Simon Peter's life came later that night. As Jesus warned the little group of friends that he was about to be arrested, Peter insisted that he would never leave Jesus. He assured Jesus that although the others might abandon him, Jesus could count on him to stay at his side. By this time, Jesus knew Simon well enough to predict that he would be the first to deny him. Sure enough, when the police had taken Jesus, several people claimed to recognize Simon Peter as one of his friends. Each time, Peter denied that he had ever met the man. As dawn broke, Jesus passed by and gave Peter a long and sorrowful look. Peter wept bitterly.

Yet in spite of his repeated failures, Peter kept trying and Jesus never gave up on him. After he had been raised from the dead, Jesus assured him that he was forgiven, and Peter went on to become one of the leaders of the Christian community – eventually dying for his faith.

Peter's experience is no different than that of other people who met Jesus. Although many of his associates criticized him, Jesus insisted on choosing people as they were, not as he wished they were. Many of his closest friends were people that most of us would consider unreliable or unpleasant. There were simple, uneducated fishermen who seemed to have few gifts that would make them likely companions of Jesus. There was an ex-guerrilla fighter who had belonged to one of the bands of rebels fighting against the Romans. There were former prostitutes, and traitors like Levi, the man who collected taxes for Caesar. Probably none of them would have seemed likely prospects to associate with the man we call Lord. And yet, he was not unhappy with them, and took them to be his companions on the way and the leaders of his movement.

What all those friends of Jesus had in common was that they had heard *good news*: they were chosen and accepted as they were. They did not have to pretend to be something they weren't. They needed no pretending in order to be taken into Jesus' company. No doubt his friends disappointed Jesus many times. Yet he continued to offer them his friendship and even his love. Ever since, Christians have understood his suffering and death as a sign of the good news that we are loved and accepted as we are. That is what we mean when we speak of the *Gospel*, which is simply an old English word for *good news*. It is no accident that we call the books which tell the story of Jesus the *gospels*. They are indeed good news.

§

No one in Andrew's family had ever been to college before. His sister had thought about it, but her boy friend had persuaded her to marry him as soon as she had graduated from high school. Now she was divorced and caring for two small children. Andrew's parents had made it clear that there was no money for college, and that if he wanted to go he would have to be responsible for the expenses himself. At the end of his junior year, he had taken a special exam for a scholarship, sent off the application papers, and begun the long wait.

The apartment was empty when he walked in from

school, but the mail was lying on the table just inside the door. There was a letter for him, looking ominous and important. He opened it and began to read.

"Dear Mr. Lewis:

We are happy to inform you that your scholarship application has been accepted. We are pleased to offer you the sum of twenty thousand dollars for the next four years, payable to the college of your choice in the amount of five thousand dollars per year."

There was more, but Andy could hardly read it. With a whoop, he flung open the door and ran up the stairs to the apartment where his friend Steve lived. He began to hammer on the door. "Steve! Open up! It's good news," he shouted.

§

The impulse to share good news is the most natural reaction in the world. It is easy to keep to ourselves the things that make us unhappy or ashamed, but good news is to be shared. The energy with which Andy raced to tell his news to his friends is not really so different from the energy with which Christians have always been anxious to tell other people what they have found about God. The experience of being accepted as they are was what sent those first

[144]

Christians all over the world with the message that God loved them, really loved them. They shared the story of the cross and Easter because they believed that those stories made life different. They understood that the death and life of Jesus mattered to them because these were the means for seeing what God is really like. In remembering the death of Christ, they saw real love. In recalling that Christ was raised from the dead, their life took on hope. No other experience could have made the Christian movement spread all over the world. But in fact, that is what happened. The small community of men and women who had known Jesus could not stop talking about him. More and more people began to listen to their good news and *believe* it. They found their own lives changed in the same way, as they grasped the truth that God really does love them.

Most important, they discovered that being loved and accepted gave genuine meaning to their life for the first time. What makes Christians understand that life is worth living is their experience of being loved. They also find meaning in passing on that love. Christians have never been silent about their faith. Otherwise, the movement would have died out long ago. But as individuals come to notice and observe that there really is love set loose in the world, they become agents of love.

The long story of the Christian family is a history of

great suffering and pain. Countless people who trusted what Jesus had shown them about life have had to pay the supreme sacrifice of their own death because of their faith. Yet they have done so willingly, because they have somehow seen that nothing in this world is more important than the love of God which surrounds them. That love has called them into being and has sustained their life from the day of their birth. That love will take them home at the end. Nothing else could possibly matter more. That is why Christians are not meant to be people of gloom and long faces, but of joy.

There is no greater tragedy than for human beings to despair about their life. There can be no worse agony than facing existence without hope and meaning. We can well understand why some people who have never known love might seek some other meaning in less creative ways. But we can also understand how important it is to share what we know and believe about hope. No one who has glimpsed something of the meaning which God's love can give to life dare keep silent about it. Christians are called to be people of love. If love is what makes life worth living for us, what greater opportunity can we have than to share that knowledge and love with others?

- - - - - - -

How would you act if you believed that life has no meaning or purpose?

Since it is often very hard to talk about the things that matter most to us, how would you go about helping someone else find out what gives purpose to life?

A Christian Lifestyle

Nancy closed the door of the "Golden Years Retirement Club" behind her forever. It marked the end of a chapter in her life that she would like to forget.

The trouble began two months ago, when she and several of her friends had strolled to the end of a pier that jutted out from the park into the river. They were alone. Phyllis had a joint, and they were sharing it when a young man in jeans and a T-shirt that said "Have a Nice Day" began walking towards them. A moment of panic clutched Nancy, but she soon relaxed, since he looked harmless. By the time he reached them, it was too late. "You're under arrest," he said firmly.

Then came the ride to the police station, the phone call to her parents, and the scene that followed when they all reached home. Nancy's parents had not suspected she smoked pot, and she had never even come close to being arrested before.

The day she went to court Nancy experienced a mixture of fear and surprise. Nancy and her friends had expected a fine, but instead they were sentenced to work for ten hours at a home for senior citizens. Nancy would have preferred a fine!

Every Sunday afternoon for five weeks she was to appear at Pinecrest Home for Adults. She was assigned to the club that provided recreation for the more active residents.

The first afternoon passed slowly. Nancy knew no one, and she had talked to very few old people before. She was nervous and quiet, and left with a feeling of relief. Only four more visits.

But then something happened. On her second visit, Nancy discovered she remembered several people's names, and she enjoyed calling out the numbers for Bingo. One very friendly woman named Mrs. Brenner admired the sweater Nancy was wearing, and they discussed a knitting project they could work on together. The hours passed so quickly that Nancy was surprised when it was time to go home.

Now it was all over. She could try to forget the embarrassment of what had brought her to the Pinecrest Home in the first place. No more Sunday afternoons with all those old people. Her time was her own. She was free again!

As she had prepared to leave, Mr. Forlano, the director, had seemed sad. "You know, Nancy," he told her, "you're one of the best volunteers we've ever had. Everyone has taken to you. We're going to miss you. I wish we weren't saying goodbye." Nancy remembered the tears in Mrs. Brenner's eyes when she explained that it was her last afternoon.

"But I'm free!" she said to herself. "I'm free." She paused for a few moments, then turned and opened the door. The director was at his desk just inside. "Mr. Forlano," she said, "I want to be a regular volunteer."

§

Nancy learned something very important from her work at the Retirement Club. She learned that there are actually two kinds of freedom.

The first is freedom *from* – freedom understood as liberation from circumstances which seem to be oppressive or stifling. When the people of Israel escaped from their slavery in Egypt, they were

[151]

experiencing this sort of freedom. For the first time in their lives, they knew what it was like to be rid of their burdens. Nancy discovered the same kind of freedom when she realized that she no longer had to work with the elderly people to whom she had been assigned. As long as her work was the result of a judge's sentence, she was not free to do what she wanted with her Sunday afternoons. It was only when she walked out of the club at the end of her ten hours of work that she was free from the restrictions that had dictated her sentence.

But the remarkable thing that occurred to Nancy as she left the Retirement Club was that she didn't have to leave at all. She was free from her duties, but she had also received another kind of freedom. She had freedom *for* – freedom for choosing what she would and would not do. Her decision to return to work as a volunteer represented this different kind of freedom – the freedom to choose.

Christians consider this second kind of freedom to be the most precious of God's gifts to the human family, because we share that freedom with God.

Freedom is also the basis for living as Christians in the world we call home. If we had no choices, but lived instead by instinct like other creatures, Christian faith would be irrelevant. We would not be able to respond to its promise.

Jesus not only shared his vision of the way things are with his companions; he also gave them a vision of the way things might be. The challenge to live as followers of Jesus is not only to share his way of seeing, but his way of acting. Jesus took both dimensions of our freedom with great seriousness. He insisted that every human being has the right to be free from oppression; but he also took for granted that we can be free to make choices.

The covenant between God and Israel was based on the assumption that the people of Israel were in fact free to live as God commanded. The Jewish Law was an attempt to put those commandments into a form that people could understand and choose to obey. Rabbis are Jewish teachers who devote their lives to studying the Law and its application to human life. As a rabbi, Jesus answered many questions about what it means to live as God expects. Once someone asked him, "Which of all the laws is most important?"

Jesus replied that the whole of the Jewish law could in fact be summed up in two commandments: You shall love the Lord your God with all your heart, and soul, and mind. You shall love your neighbor as yourself.

In Jesus' opinion, these two summaries said all that needs to be said about living as God intends. In his own life, Jesus put them into practice. Loving God and loving our neighbors as we love ourselves are the best uses to which we can put our freedom.

Many people find it difficult to take Jesus' words seriously, because they can't imagine how love can be a matter of choice at all. Anyone who examines the way he or she feels at any given moment soon realizes that our feelings don't always obey us. Instead, they seem to have a life of their own. We are shocked to find ourselves angry, bored, or excited when we least expect it. Sometimes we can't even be sure of why we feel the way we do. "Did you get up on the wrong side of bed this morning?" your mother asks as you appear at the breakfast table with a frown on your face. And even if you wanted to explain why you feel wretched, you can't really put it into words. That's the way feelings are. They don't disappear or change on command, even when they get in our way and we wish we could be rid of them.

But if feelings are beyond our control, then how can Jesus command us to love?

Jesus was not talking about love as a feeling, but as a way of behaving. We have no choice about how we feel, but we do have freedom to act in one way or another. Greek, the language in which the New Testament was written, has several words which we translate as "love." One is the kind of love we mean when we speak of physical passion between two people. Another was reserved for the love between friends. A third, which is the word writers of the New Testament chose in passing on Jesus' teachings, appears over and over in the Scriptures. In Greek, the word is *agape*. Its special meaning is actually closer to what we mean in English by *respect* than what we usually mean by *love*. You might even rephrase Jesus' command to read: "Respect your neighbor as you respect yourself." Understood in that way, Jesus' commandment is not talking about feelings at all, but about a way of behaving towards other people which gives them the respect we ask for ourselves.

Self-respect is actually the beginning of love as Jesus understood it. The attitude we have towards ourselves determines the way we treat other people. Christians respect themselves because they understand that they have been created in the image of God, and because they grasp something of the truth that God loves them and accepts them just as they are. You might say that self-respect is the first result of the Good News as Christians believe it.

But if that Good News gives us self-respect, it is also the basis for the respect we owe others. We accept their right to be treated with dignity simply because they are also loved and accepted by God, and because they too are created in God's image.

This awareness of the right of every human being to

be treated with dignity and respect often sets Christians off from others who do not share their way of looking at things. Some societies ignore or mistreat people who do not measure up to what is considered to be worthy of the status of first-class citizenship. Some of the worst examples of human cruelty have come when the basic right to human dignity is denied. The Holocaust, in which millions of Jews and members of other groups were slaughtered during the Second World War, shows all too clearly what can happen when people fail to love their neighbors as they love themselves. Slavery and segregation are other examples of what can happen when people deny to others the respect they assume for themselves. But we might also ask ourselves what are the implications of Jesus' teaching about dignity in situations much closer to home. Is respect always shown to old people in nursing homes, patients in mental hospitals, inmates in prison, or to poor people who are condemned through no fault of their own to live in slums?

- - - - - - -

What might be the consequences if we took seriously the right of all people to be treated with dignity and respect?

- - - - - - -

After he broke his back in a car accident, Gerald

spent many weeks in the hospital. When he began to feel a little better, the advisor of his youth group came to see him. She brought a large notebook with her. "I thought you might like to have this," she said. "When I was sick a couple of years ago, someone suggested that I keep a journal, and it really helped me a lot. I used to write in it when I was feeling low, and now when I read it I find it helps me remember what it was like, and to hold on to what I learned when I was sick."

At first, Gerald thought it was a useless idea. He had never liked writing for English classes, and it seemed strange to write anything when you didn't have to. But one night his back began to ache especially badly, and he picked up the notebook. "It feels as if my spine is on fire," he wrote. It was the first line of his journal.

As time went by, Gerald came to rely on his notebook. Hardly a day passed when he did not find himself adding thoughts to it several times. Once he went home he got out of the habit, but he still kept his journal hidden under his mattress, ready whenever he wanted to put into words something he couldn't share with anyone.

One day, Gerald walked into the living room. His mother was sitting there, reading what looked like his journal.

"What is that?" he asked.

"It's the book you had under your mattress," she replied. "I found it while I was changing your bed. You forgot to give me your sheets this morning. You know it's laundry day."

"You read my journal!" Gerald shouted. "I can't believe it. You read my journal!"

"Oh, for heaven's sake," his mother answered. "There's nothing in it to be ashamed of. In fact, it's pretty good. You ought to show it to Fr. Gresham and your English teacher. I think they'd be very interested in it."

"You read my journal!" Gerald shouted again, and went outside, slamming the door.

- - - - - - -

Was Gerald right to be angry at his mother? Why or why not?

- - - - - - -

Most people would probably agree that Gerald's mother failed to respect her son's privacy when she read a journal which was clearly meant to be private. Christians believe that the respect which human

[158]

beings owe to one another is the basis of every human relationship. Love between members of a family has very little meaning unless it is translated into genuine respect.

But the same respect is meant to govern all relationships between people. Friendship really depends on whether or not two people consider each other as worthy of being treated with dignity just because they are who they are. If we allow our behavior to be determined by what we think we may get from someone, we are not really friends at all. We are simply using another person – the best example of how *not* to treat another human being with respect.

§

"I want to go home."

"Oh, come on, Carol, I'm sorry. I didn't think you'd take it that way."

"I'm serious, Bill, I want you to take me home."

"But Carol, I love you."

"You don't love me, Bill, you just want me. You don't respect me at all."

"Please, Bill, take me home."

[159]

A Christian Lifestyle

§

Probably no aspect of human experience illustrates better the difference between love as a feeling and what Christians mean by love than sexuality. Christians believe that sexual relations are part of the gift of creation which God gives us. Sexuality is holy, because it is a means by which two human beings express their commitment to each other. Such love is, we believe, a reflection of the love of God. In the love between a husband and wife, we can see a sign of the love which Jesus has for the world and all its people.

The impulse to form sexual relationships is one of the strongest desires we know – stronger than any other except the need for food and drink. Sexuality induces emotions that seem almost overpowering. Many people assume that these strong sexual feelings are, in fact, love. Most popular music is written on the assumption that love is a matter of being sexually and romantically attracted. We live in a culture that takes for granted that love and sex are the same thing. "I love you" can usually be translated, "I am sexually attracted to you."

Christians, however, approach sex very differently. We know just as well as anyone else the strength of sexual feelings. We know too that there is nothing we can do about those feelings. We cannot turn them off, nor can we dictate to our emotions whom we are going to find attractive.

But our emotions do not dictate how we behave. What we *feel* is beyond our control; how we *act* is a matter of choice and freedom. Christians believe that because it is holy, sex is not to be taken lightly or as a form of recreation but as an act of genuine commitment between two people who have profound respect for each other. Without respect, no sexual relationship could ever be called love as Christians understand the word.

- - - - - - -

Do you think that Bill really loved Carol?

What would be loving behavior in their situation?

- - - - - - -

Love based on human dignity is the basis for all human life as Christians try to live it. It provides a model for the way groups and nations coexist with one another. History tells many tales of the countless ways by which people have imposed their will on others. The long legacy of war and violence which has haunted the human race can be understood as the failure of respect, of love as Jesus understood it. If nations and peoples genuinely believed in the dignity of all human life, they would never behave towards others in the ways that we know in fact they do. How could people who see the image of God in each human being ever practice torture or consider nuclear war? If all human life is infinitely valuable in God's eyes, how can people devise systems which guarantee that some people dominate and oppress others? How can Christians, who believe in the equal dignity of every human life, stand idly by or remain silent while millions of adults and children suffer hunger, pain, separation and even death? The challenge to respect the dignity of every human person makes us uncomfortable in the face of the many examples we all know in which human life is devalued or degraded.

§

"Catherine!"

With a start, Catherine looked up from her homework and out the window, which opened onto the patio.

"José!" she exclaimed. "What are you doing here?"

She had known him for nearly a year now, at least well enough to greet when she met him at church. He had appeared just before Christmas, and she had noticed him doing all sorts of odd jobs: sweeping the sidewalk early on Sunday morning, mowing the lawn, even loading the bird feeder that hung outside the parish house door. At first, he had hardly spoken English at all, but lately she had noticed how much more easily he was able to communicate with everyone. He really seemed to be at home. But Catherine was surprised to find him outside her window.

"Catherine! I need your help!" There was no mistaking the fear in his voice.

Catherine put a bookmark in her book and left the room. In a moment she was outside on the patio with José. "What is it? What's the matter?"

"There's something you don't know about me," he began. "I came to this country without permission."

Catherine was shocked. Although she had heard about illegal immigrants before, she had certainly never imagined that she knew anyone who fit that description. "But why did you do that?" she asked.

"My family are *campesinos*, country people," he explained. We lived up in the mountains of my country, and we worked for a very rich man who owns all the land for miles around my village. He is the cousin of the general who controls my country."

A Christian Lifestyle

Catherine recalled the time José had spoken to her youth group about Central America. He had told them he was twenty-two years old, and had come to the United States years before with his parents. She remembered being surprised at the time that he was so old; he seemed closer to her own age, five years younger. She wondered too why he had not learned English if he had been here so long.

"What I told the youth group wasn't exactly true," he went on. "My father and his neighbors tried to organize the coffee pickers in our village because they could no longer feed their families on the money they were making. One day the soldiers came. They burned our house and they shot my father and my older brother. My mother told me to run away, because she was afraid they would come again and kill us all."

Catherine could hardly believe what José was telling her. She had heard stories like his on the news, but it always seemed so far away. Now José told her the long story of how he had escaped, how he had made his way by night across the border, how he had found his job at the church and a room with a family from his own country.

"Now I need your help," he repeated. "This morning when I came to work, there was a police car in front of the church. I waited outside until they left. The secretary told me they had been asking questions about me. Catherine, if they catch me, they will send me back to my country. I will surely be killed."

"But why would they send you away?" Catherine asked.

"Because I entered your country illegally," José answered.

"But you were running for your life."

"That doesn't matter. If I don't have permission to stay here, the police will send me back to my own country."

"Why would they kill you there? You haven't done anything wrong."

"That doesn't matter. My family was trying to help change things. They were trying to make a better life for us. They thought they could struggle for a little more justice. But in my country, such things are dangerous. Catherine, I will never forget the sight of my father's body lying beside that of my brother."

"What do you want me to do?" Catherine asked doubtfully.

José nodded towards the garage. "Let me stay there for a few days, until the police stop looking for me. Then I will be able to leave town with more safety."

Catherine felt a spasm of fear. She knew that what José was asking her to do was against the law. If he were caught there, she would be in trouble – not only with her parents, but just as certainly with the police. She could be arrested herself. Her parents would be involved, too.

"Why did you come here?" she asked.

"I remembered when I talked to the young people at the church. You asked most of the questions, and you seemed to care about what was happening in my country. I told myself that day that if I ever needed help, I would come to you."

Catherine looked at his face, pained, pleading. She could really not conceive of what it must be like to remember what he remembered. He said nothing more, but his eyes looked at her without flinching. She imagined trying to explain to her parents why José was staying in the garage; imagined what she would say to the police if they should come to the door. José was still looking at her, waiting for her answer. There was very little time. She had to decide.

- - - - - - -

What would you do if you were in Catherine's situation? Why?

What are the *issues* involved in her choice?

Does being a Christian give you any resources for making decisions like Catherine's?

- - - - - - -

Being a Christian means living with our freedom as sons and daughters of a God who has made us brothers and sisters. We are aware that the vision of the human family which would come into being if dignity were to prevail is a long way from reality. Most of us have trouble even remembering to behave with respect towards those who are closest to us. We fail again and again. Sometimes we even forget to respect ourselves. We overlook the image of God that we bear in ourselves. How much harder it is to live in our complicated world as people who take freedom and human dignity seriously. How seldom we remember.

But we keep on trying. Even when others shrug their shoulders and give up in despair, the Christian community continues to hold up a model of human life in which respect is not just a pious ideal, but a way of living. We Christians continue to recall that Jesus once lived such a life. In spite of our failures, we keep trying.

A Christian is not a finished product, but a living human being who is constantly growing and changing, failing, and starting over again. Christians know they are a part of a community with memories and hopes. They often have questions and doubts. Just when things seem to make sense, something new and unexpected happens and then it seems as if nothing at all makes sense.

Nor does becoming a Christian happen once and for all. We enter the community of the followers of Jesus when we are baptized, but that is not the end; it is only the beginning. It is the work of a lifetime to follow the way of Jesus. There are detours on the way, and dead ends. Sometimes there are accidents and disasters. The road leads through deserts when our loneliness is almost overwhelming. There are dark nights, full of strange and unseen dangers and terrifying nightmares. There are magnificent mornings when everything seems bright. Storms come and go, and the road may be blocked by obstacles which seem to last forever. But the figure of Jesus remains on the horizon, beckoning us to follow him, and promising that if we do, we won't be disappointed.

The first Christians called themselves "followers of the Way." To undertake the journey of faith requires commitment, not just once, but again and again. But for two thousand years, Christians have believed that it is worth the price. It is the way that gives meaning to life. It is the way of love.

INDEX